ILSA Guide
to
International Law Moot Court Competition

ILSA Guide

to

International Law Moot Court Competition

Cecilie Elisabeth Schjatvet and Zakir Hafez

A Publication of the
International Law Students Association

INTERNATIONAL LAW INSTITUTE

ISBN 0-935328-94-7

Manufactured in the United States of America

Table of Contents

Contents

A Word from the International Law Students Association

Inasmuch as this book was inspired by the authors' participation in the Philip C. Jessup International Law Moot Court Competition, a couple of words about the Jessup Competition at the outset are in order.

The Jessup Competition is a world-wide moot court competition, bringing together teams of law students to brief and argue issues of public international law. The Jessup is based upon a hypothetical fact pattern, the Compromis, which lays out a dispute between two fictional states. Teams of law students prepare written and oral arguments for both sides in the case, for presentation before a simulated International Court of Justice. Recent Jessup problems have focused on issues including the repatriation of cultural property, extradition of international criminals, international adoption law, transboundary environmental disputes, and international Internet law.

In 2002, teams from 386 law schools in 65 countries participated in the Jessup, making it the largest moot court competition in the world. These teams competed in the first instance in various Regional and National Competitions, held in January and February. The champions of each of these preliminary competitions were invited to participate in the International Rounds, held for a week in March in Washington, D.C. In 2002, 75 teams participated in the International Rounds.

The events of the past fifteen years, including the end of the Cold War and the events of and after September 11, 2001, have resulted in a dramatic increase in interest in international law. Consequently, the Jessup has undergone considerable growth. Each year, dozens of new teams—and new countries—participate in the Jessup for the first time.

This influx of new teams is the impetus for this book. Teams at schools or in countries with no tradition of moot court—or with only recent introduction to public international law—frequently find themselves at a distinct disadvantage in the Jessup. It has long been thought by the Jessup community that an introductory book, giving the first-time competitor an idea of the basics of international law, international mooting, and the Jessup in particular, would give new competitors a level of comfort with the Competition.

The authors have prepared this book from their own experiences, and in consultation with other Jessup and international law experts. However, the methodologies and strategies in this book should not be considered canonical. Each team—and each participant—should feel free to modify these techniques to fit their own resources and skills.

ILSA would like to thank Ms. Schjatvet and Mr. Hafez for all of their hard work. ILSA would also like to thank all of the teams, competitors, and volunteers who have made the Jessup Competition what it is today. If you have any questions or comments about this volume, please feel free to contact ILSA at ILSA@ILSA.ORG.

Michael Peil
Executive Director
International Law Students Association

Foreword

More than 40 years after the birth of the prestigious Philip C. Jessup International Law Moot Court Competition, an indispensable resource for Jessup competitors has arrived—the *ILSA Guide to International Law Moot Court Competitions*, by former Jessup competitors Cecilie Elisabeth Schjatvet and Zakir Hafez. The *Guide*, which provides a methodical approach to research, drafting, writing style, and oral argument, will lead the new team member comfortably through what at first seems a daunting experience.

Law students in the United States have long had a broad variety of persuasive writing and oral argument texts to rely upon as they prepare for their moot court experience. International law moot court competitors, however, have had to extrapolate from traditional texts, which deal with, typically, domestic United States law rather than international law. Ms. Schjatvet's and Mr. Hafez's book, however, puts persuasive writing and oral argument into the international law context, providing the reader with basic concepts of international legal terminology and research *integrated with* principles of persuasive writing and oral advocacy. The authors also set forth fundamental concepts of international law that competitors may use as a starting point for their research.

The *ILSA Guide* presupposes the reader's basic knowledge of international law. Building upon that foundation, the authors offer a unique suggestion for Jessup competitors—drafting preliminary research memoranda on the various issues raised by the *compromis*, the agreement that brings an international dispute before the moot International Court of Justice. This approach should guarantee that the competitors are thoroughly grounded in their research before they convert their memoranda into strong, persuasive memorials to submit to the Court.

Throughout, the authors provide the reader with examples drawn from actual Jessup Competition briefs and oral arguments to create a realistic setting for the competitors. The competitors are reminded of one of the basic principles of effective brief writing and oral advocacy—to keep the audience in mind.

Competitors will find most helpful the authors' strategies for rules of international law in their memorials and especially the sections on oral advocacy, usually the most thrilling but most nerve-wracking part of the moot court experience. Ms. Schjatvet and Mr. Hafez offer numerous practical tips for organizing and presenting oral argument effectively that should make the competitor feel confident as the moment of competition nears. The reader is, of course, always free to pick and choose portions of the *Guide* or to use it as a whole in preparation for competition.

This book will be a welcome addition to the resources of Jessup competitors and their coaches and advisors. The authors' user-friendly style and step-by-step approach should be helpful to the more than a thousand competitors from over fifty countries that compete in the Jessup each year. Most important, the *Guide* can help to make this exciting competition easier to prepare for and a more enjoyable experience.

Diane Penneys Edelman
Assistant Dean for Legal Writing
Villanova University School of Law

Preface

This is a hands-on book that we trust will be useful for students, coaches and faculty advisors involved in a wide variety of moot-court experiences. For participants who have no previous experience with international law moot courts, this serves as a primer, introducing the topics of moot court, international law, and oral and legal advocacy. For participants with prior coursework in international law, it provides a guide for applying this knowledge to the moot-court context. For participants with competition experience, it provides a first glimpse into how moot court differs when the legal basis is international law. And finally, for those with experience with international law moot courts, this text is intended to serve as a ready guidebook, for "refreshers" on certain topics and for quick reference. The book focuses on process and structure, and strives to illustrate with examples. The intention is to function as a road map in the students' research and writing process.

This is not a textbook in international law. A basic understanding of international law is presupposed for working with this book. The reference to principles of international law throughout the book is not to be viewed as a discussion of the principles, but rather as a link to accelerate the thought process and the development of the task at hand.

The presentation of the material is not intended for professional use. Moot court is a pedagogical exercise, designed to focus students on certain elements of bringing a case to court. This handbook is written with this approach, rather than that of the practicing attorney, in mind.

Although this book is intended for students of any nationality, it is written in English. This is because the working language of many international tribunals, and most international-law moot court competitions, is English. Considering the level of English proficiency among university students, this should not pose a barrier to non-native speakers of English.

There is a dearth of publicly available material concerning preparation for international law moot courts. Therefore, in the preparing for this project, we consulted the existing reference materials, which focus primarily on the body of literature that exists on the subject within the context of U.S. domestic law. First and foremost however, we wrote this book on the basis of our experience participating and coaching in international law moot court competition. We welcome any reactions the readers might have on the content or the material of this book.

We wish to extend our gratitude to Dr. Juris Geir Ulfstein at the University of Oslo, for supervising the project. We are also indebted to both Dr. Juris Geir Ulfstein and to Rita Kilvær, team member on the Norwegian Jessup team 1999, for their thoughtful and valuable comments on our manuscript. We would also like to thank the participants at the weekly luncheons on international law at the Institute for Public and International Law at the University of Oslo.

In Washington D.C., we are grateful to Professor Raj Bhala, Professor Ralph Steinhardt, Dean Michael Young, Dean Susan Karamanian, Edward Krauland, Thomas Graham, James Jones, Joseph Brand, John Magnus, John Ragosta, Kara Tan Bhala, Shera Tan Bhala, Noman Hafez, and Anne Seymour for their help and encouragement. Of course, our largest debt of gratitude is to Michael Peil, Executive Director of the International Law Students Association, for carefully editing and reviewing the manuscript. And, we specially thank the International Law Institute for publishing the book.

Finally, we welcome any and all constructive comments and suggestions in order to improve the product. Please direct these comments to us by e-mail: Cecilie Schjatvet at *cecilie.schjatvet@hestenesdramer.no.*; Zakir Hafez at *Zakir@gwu.edu.*

Cecilie Elisabeth Schjatvet and Zakir Hafez

CHAPTER 1

Introduction

I.   Characteristics of International Law Moot Court Competitions

As the name implies, an "international-law moot court" is a simulation of legal practice before an international court, usually the International Court of Justice or some regional human-rights tribunal. The case is typically based upon a hypothetical set of facts (the "Compromis") and involves two fictional state parties. International law moot court gives you an opportunity to analyze, research, write and argue a single, fictional case before a model international court. In a well-written Compromis, the legal issues presented involve—at least in part—problems that are disputed or not resolved in international law.

    In international law moot court, developing the case requires you to write research papers, draft a Memorial, and present an oral argument based on the Memorial before a bench of law professors, judges or practicing lawyers.

II. The Purpose of International Law Moot Court Competitions

International law moot court might be the only law course in which you are asked to act as though you were a practicing international-law attorney.

There are a number of professional and academic advantages to such an experience.

A. The art of analysis

1. Law without facts is a theoretical matter

The traditional classroom-based legal education does not focus on facts in solving legal problems. The emphasis is typically on the academic points of the law. In moot court, the student must manage the law to fit the facts. You are required to select and apply legal principles to the facts presented, rather than performing the strictly academic exercise of remembering and reciting a rule. This is not to say that your academic training does not play an important role. On the contrary, the difficulties inherent in interpreting the possible outcomes of a complicated statute or an indeterminate contract become all the more important when you are representing a party.

2. Synthesis

In all likelihood, you have probably spent much of your time identifying the rule of law as construed in a given statute or a case. If the law is uncertain in a particular situation, it is usually sufficient to identify the problem and make suggestions as to how to interpret or amend the law. In international law moot court, you will be asked to act as a lawyer. You must take the law for what it is, and present arguments in support of your client's case. The sources need to be synthesized, even if directly applicable law is missing. In international law, this exercise is especially important: the law can be stated in several treaties, in customary international law, and in different principles. In developing your case, you will acquire analytical skills that will help you present and interpret the rules you need to support your case.

3. In-depth exposure to legal questions

In law school courses, analysis of legal problems is necessarily limited by available class time. In international law moot court, you will have the opportunity to spend enough time on the problem to appreciate the complexity of legal questions.

B.   Research skills

One of the most significant skills a young attorney can develop is the ability to determine the law. This entails a capacity to decide what law is relevant in light of a proper analysis of the facts. Developing this skill is a central part of your preparation for international law moot court.

C.   Writing and speaking skills

The typical law school examination requires you merely to present arguments for both sides in a given case in an objective manner. In actual practice, however, lawyers are required to distinguish between writing to persuade and writing merely to describe. Writing persuasively requires you to take a position, and to anticipate and rebut your counter-arguments. International law moot court gives you such an opportunity to write persuasively.

International law moot court gives you an opportunity to develop and test your oral advocacy skills. Whatever you are planning to do with your legal education, developing oral skills in a legal context will prove indispensable to your future work.

III. Succeeding in International Law Moot Court Competitions

International law moot court is a different experience than the theoretical approaches of other subjects. The experience will prove to be a positive one. Most students feel excitement at the prospect of doing something "real" and eagerly anticipate the adventure of the oral argument.

But like all new experiences, moot court may cause anxiety. Accept these feelings as normal and genuine. Quite a few of us tend to feel alienated in a library. To dread the arduousness of the writing process is common, as most writers like to "get it right" the first time. Many people are uncertain about their qualities as speakers and fear public speaking. Frequently, your research does not leave you with authorities that fit your facts. Group discussions among your fellow team members on the issues may prove challenging when there exists no supreme authority to decide who is right and who is wrong. You may feel that you have taken on tasks that are impossible to complete.

A key to understanding international law moot court is that the uncertainty of the law is intended to be your point of departure. You have been given an opportunity to develop confidence in your skills as a lawyer.

As you realize that you really have researched all the sources that are likely to produce results, the sense of intimidation passes. When the time comes to make your oral presentation, you may in fact find that you know the applicable law better than the judges. When it is all over, most students are left with a feeling of excitement and wish to do it again.

IV. Using This Handbook

Most moot court problems fit a certain pattern. This handbook is designed to serve as a road map in your quest for the finished Memorial and the final oral presentation.

Remember that there is no one correct way to write a Memorial or argue a case. The experienced advocate might find the approach presented in this handbook to be too declaratory. The specific suggestions in this presentation are not intended to exclude other approaches, but to present one approach that has proven to be effective.

V. Methodology of Law and International Law

The methodology of law is a necessary part of any legal system. The difference between the international system and domestic systems is significant when considering the approach to research and writing. Before turning to the specifics of the international law moot court, one central point must be emphasized.

The methodology of international law has often been characterized as reflecting a legal positivist view of legal sources. The often-proclaimed division of principal and subsidiary sources, and the sometimes-used distinction between "hard law" and "soft law" reflects this view. Although it may be a safe assumption to apply this approach to the sources when doing research in international law, it is not necessarily an accurate one. There are good arguments to be made that application of international law is a process where context is important. For the purposes of this text, it is not necessary to decide between these two viewpoints. Although it is useful to be aware of the divergence of thought, it is sufficient at this time to simply identify the problem and state that there are several viable views on how to describe the methodology of the argument in international law.

VI. Some Notes About Vocabulary

International law moot court has a vocabulary of its own. Much of the terminology is derived from the practice of the International Court of Justice. This handbook adopts the terminology of the largest international law competitions. Students should familiarize themselves with the following terms, both in using this handbook and in practicing before the (mock) Court.

- The statement of facts in the case is called the "Compromis."
- The parties to the case, which are typically states, are the "Applicant" and the "Respondent."
- The written argument (which you will prepare) is called the "Memorial"
- The chairman (or chair-woman) of the Court is the "President," and is typically addressed as "Madam President" or "Mister President."
- The other members of the Court are "Justices," and are typically addressed as "Justice [last name]." The President or the justices may also be referred to as "Your Excellency" (when addressed) or "His Excellency" or "Her Excellency" (when talked about).

CHAPTER 2

Analysis of the Compromis

I.   Some Characteristics of the Compromis

The statement of facts, or Compromis, is the source of information about the facts of the case. While you will read many pages on the law, the facts are contained solely within the 10 to 15 pages of the Compromis. Therefore, this brief statement of the facts deserves a close analysis.

The Compromis presents the factual basis of the case before the Court. The Compromis is a negotiated statement whereby the parties submit themselves to the jurisdiction of the court, pursuant to Article 36 of the Statute of the International Court of Justice (ICJ). Every sentence in the Compromis is drafted in a way that is acceptable to both of the parties to the case. For this reason, you must be careful to respect the scope of the facts to which both parties have agreed. Do not "invent" new facts to fill in apparent gaps in the Compromis—if the parties wanted to include a particular fact, they would have included it in the Compromis. Taking this into account, however, there are still many interpretations to any set of facts. Creatively interpreting the facts can be the key to developing the approach that can help the judge solve the case.

Context and background have a substantial effect on the meaning and importance of any given fact. Effective interpretation of the facts can improve the case before research of the law has even begun. This Chapter will develop your understanding of the context of the facts and their importance to the legal issues of the case before your research in the library has even started.

Keep in mind that facts are dynamic. The process of matching the law and the facts is ongoing. By determining the context of the facts, your initial research will be more narrowly focused and better encompass all the issues. As you become more familiar with the law, you will alter your perception of the facts. Remember that the law drives the facts and the facts drive the law.

In the following example, *Case Concerning the Football League (Sucsdesh v. Takkistan)*, a three-step approach of analyzing the facts is presented. It focuses on a case that is much shorter than the typical Compromis, but serves as an example for application of the principles of factual interpretation.

> The Quinns are an ethnic group whose culture is centered in the Kingdom of Takkistan. One million Quinns also live in the Republic of Sucsdesh, which is in the same geographical region as Takkistan.
>
> The ethnic composition of Sucsdesh is 20% Quinns and 70% Isis. The Isis hold a large majority in the legislature. Since its independence in 1990, Sucsdesh has denied Quinns the right to form a separate football league. In 1998, Takkistan sponsored an all-Quinnian Football Cup in Sucsdesh. At the preliminary rounds of the cup, participants for Quinn interest groups held speeches, agitating for a separate Quinn government within the territory of Sucsdesh within one year. The Sucsdeshian police moved to close down the sporting arrangement and dispersed the participants. An International Humanitarian Watch Group reported that many Quinns were wounded and that 20 died. Takkistan protested to Sucsdesh, stating that the Quinns were denied freedom of speech and association. The Sucsdeshian Government replied that gathering at the Football League was illegal, and that the Constitution of 1996 did not allow for separatist ideologies. After inconclusive exchanges of diplomatic notes, the parties agreed to submit their disputes to the International Court of Justice pursuant to article 36(1) of the Court's Statute.

II. Analyze the Facts in the Compromis

Using the *Case Concerning the Football League* as a basis, analyze the facts in the Compromis, following the steps outlined below.

Get to know your facts

The first step is to organize the facts into logical categories, to determine what the case is all about. In "getting to know your facts," you can look at one state at a time, or consider the perspectives simultaneously. In later phases of your preparation, you will represent one side or another; therefore, it is important to approach the problem at this stage with an unbiased perspective. Bear in mind, however, that keeping the interests of both sides is important even at later stages of research, in the writing of the Memorial and in preparing your oral presentation.

1.   What happened and when did it happen?

During your first review of the Compromis, note all the turning points in the Compromis, as they will show what happened. The facts in a Compromis are not necessarily arranged in chronological order. Preparing a chronology of events will give you a comprehensive and detailed understanding of the factual setting, because a case may turn not on what happened, but when it happened.

In *the Case Concerning the Football League*, an important issue in determining whether Takkistan unlawfully interfered in Sucsdesh's affairs may be Sucsdesh's reference to its Constitution of 1996. A reading of the Compromis shows that the Quinn minority in Sucsdesh was denied a separate football league since its independence in 1990. This is important, because if denial of the right to freedom of assembly was also denied before the Constitution was revised, Sucsdesh is less likely to successfully claim that the speeches were illegal according to their Constitution.

2.   Where did it happen? Who acted and how was it done?

Where an event happened can in some instances be of greater interest than what or when it happened. You might, for example, map the geographical distances between the two countries and the events of the Compromis, as the geographical distances can sometimes determine the significance of what happened.

In the *Case Concerning the Football League*, an important issue is whether Takkistan has unlawfully supported separatist activities in Sucsdesh. A reading of the facts shows that Takkistan is in the same region as Sucsdesh, which might be important in demonstrating Takkistan's motivation for involvement with a minority group in another country.

In your map and your chronology, indicate the actors. Identify them by name and background. Who acted, state officials or private individuals? Did some individual, group or institution benefit from the act?

In the *Case Concerning the Football League*, determining who acted is necessary in order for Takkistan to succeed in claiming Sucsdesh violated the rights of the Quinns, as the violations must be attributable to the state.

Also, indicate in a diagram and chronology some description of how the events happened. In what way did the turning points happen? Were the acts perpetrated through force or violence?

In the *Case Concerning the Football League*, the level of force involved is important in supporting Takkistan's claim that Sucsdesh has violated the Quinns' rights to freedom of speech and association.

3. Why did it happen?

Now, make suggestions as to why the facts happened the way they did. This is important in determining the effect of one state's actions or omissions upon the other. Using your chronology, identify the motivation or causes of each action in the Compromis. What alternative routes of action did the parties have? What events in the Compromis were outside the control of the parties?

For instance, in the *Case Concerning the Football League*, could Sucsdesh have met their concerns about Quinn separatism by other means than dispersing the meetings? The dispersing of the crowd at the Football Cup was the first event that led to alleged casualties and injuries. The sponsoring of the Football Cup could have encouraged more resistance in the Quinns, but the violent incident could have been the result of ten years of discrimination.

4. Which events or details are likely to be given more weight than other items?

Consider the varying importance the court is likely to attach to each fact. The Court does not review the facts that are stipulated by both parties and are undisputed. The Court, however, must review the facts presented by either party, by a witness or an interest group. To anticipate the Court's review, consider the basis for a party's refusal to accept the findings.

For instance, in the *Case Concerning the Football League*, the fact that the Quinns held political speeches at the Football Cup is undisputed. On the other hand, an International Humanitarian Watch Group reported the alleged casualties and injuries. If the Court can consider the reports of international watch groups as factual findings, Takkistan may be more successful in claiming that Sucsdesh violated human rights.

5. What facts are "missing"?

In conducting an analysis of the facts, you will also discover that some facts are missing or ambiguous. Remember that this is probably intentional. Where the Compromis is silent, attempts to determine what happened amount to speculation, as the Compromis is an agreement between the parties. You are not permitted by the Court (or the rules of your Competition) to engage in mere speculation. You are, however, allowed to make necessary inferences from the available facts. A necessary inference is an inference from items in the facts that lead to only one conclusion. Be aware that misuse of facts in your Memorial or your oral presentation will hurt your credibility with the Court.

You are permitted, however, to determine the practical implications of why certain facts are absent. For example, in the *Case Concerning the Football League*, the Compromis fails to indicate to what extent the speeches on the Quinns' right to self-determination agitated for violent measures. This is important, because if the speeches agitated for violent measures, Sucsdesh would be more likely to succeed in its claim that it was justified in dispersing the meeting. If not, Sucsdesh is left in the difficult position of arguing that simply spreading the idea of a separate Quinn government within the territory of Sucsdesh does not fall within the ambit of the international legal right to self-determination.

Also consider which slight alterations of the facts that could alter the outcome of the case dramatically. The judge may give different weight to facts that are, on the one hand, completely unique to the case and, on the other hand, facts that reflect recurring situations in international affairs. Although ICJ cases do not have strict precedental value, states use decisions of the Court in guiding future conduct. Therefore, a judge will apply rules with one eye on future situations where the rule may be invoked.

In the *Case Concerning the Football League*, the prohibition of separatist ideologies in Sucsdesh's Constitution can be found in many constitutions around the world. On the other hand, Sucsdesh's restriction of its football league to one ethnic group is quite unique. It demands consideration of the importance of the right of an ethnic group to have access to a football league, and invites parallels to the rights ethnic groups usually claim for themselves.

III. Identify Topical Issues

A. Determine the meaning of words and phrases

By now, you will have a solid grasp of the different aspects of the story in the Compromis. You may, however, not have an accurate understanding of the significance of the words and phrases used. Even if you believe you know the conventional meaning of a word, be sure to consult a legal dictionary concerning key words and phrases to understand the legal definition of the words.

B. Determine areas that might require further inquiries

A case may concern areas of life with which you are unfamiliar. In the *Football League* case, you probably do not need to make further inquiries on the specifics of national and international football leagues. However, a case that concerns cancellation of contracts may require you to inquire about how book value is determined. If the case involves the improper use of a particular equipment or tool, you should familiarize yourself with the equipment's conventional uses, limitations and possibilities.

IV. Connect the Facts to the Legal Issues

The key to an effective argument will be your ability to relate the legal arguments to the specific factual situation. Before heading to the library, make a preliminary assessment of which facts are most important to each issue. The process of relating the facts to the law is of course continuous, and determining which facts apply to the law is the first step in this process. Two possible approaches to organizing your research are suggested here:

A. The topic approach

One approach is to identify the general legal topic involved in each issue. For instance, you may determine that the legal topic underlying Sucsdesh's interference in Quinnian political activities is freedom of speech or assembly. This is a topic with which you may be familiar from your courses concerning domestic law. However, identifying some topics may require specific knowledge of international law. For this reason you may find it useful to use the index approach to determine the topic.

B. The index approach — TARP

Another approach is to conduct a search based on specific facts. To employ the index approach, identify, if possible, the thing involved (T), the act that gave rise to the action (A), the relief sought (R), and the persons involved (P). The purpose is to search sources of international law for the words you determine by the TARP formula. You may proceed in the following manner:

(i) *Relief sought.* Start with the relief sought. At the end of the Compromis, there are one or two paragraphs that list the specific action the parties want the Court to take; these are the "requests for relief." The parties' requests may be ambiguous, and a closer reading of the facts may be required to determine the basis and specifics of the claims.

(ii) *Persons involved.* Identify the persons involved in the claim. In this case it is the Quinns. In other cases, you may identify other classes of people, such as minors, professionals, or people in a certain relationship, like that between the diplomat and the state.

(iii) *The act.* Identify the act that gave rise to the claim. In this case, it was the organization of the all-Quinn Football Cup where the speeches were held. In other cases a natural catastrophe, a speech, or any of a number of events may be the reason for the act.

(iv) *Thing involved.* Identify the thing involved by deciding which object is central to the facts that gives rise to the relief sought. It may be as different as a ship, a bomb or a computer. In this case, no "thing" can be naturally described as a thing involved in the act.

Thus, the following (underlined) words could be the vantage points for an index search in sources of international law:

Key index research words—TARP approach:

— *the football cup (<u>sports arrangement</u>) (T)*
— *organizing minority activities (the <u>speeches</u>) (A)*
— *support for <u>self-determination</u> is illegal (R)*
— *the <u>minority group</u>, the Quinns (P)*

CHAPTER 3

Writing Preliminary Research Papers

This Chapter concerns the elements of a preliminary legal research paper. Although this Chapter presupposes some research, this Chapter is placed ahead of the Chapters on how to do research in order to help you formulate your research strategy. Familiarizing yourself with the requirements of a research paper before starting your research will save time. It will prevent you from having to revisit your research.

I.   The Purpose of the Legal Research Paper

A legal research paper is a summary of the law relevant to the issues you identified at the end of your evaluation of the Compromis. Legal research papers are written for a variety of purposes and in a variety of formats. In preparing for an international law moot court, a properly written research paper serves as the foundation for writing a Memorial. To this end, it will accomplish four main tasks.

First, writing the research paper will give you an overview of the legal issues. Second, in writing the research paper you will write objectively. Objective writing will familiarize you with the strong and weak arguments of both sides. Third, the conclusions of your research paper will direct your further research. Your will discover how the different legal conclusions do or do not fit the facts, which sources are conflicting, and which are ambiguous. Fourth, assuming you are using a proper footnote system, writing the research paper will provide a record of the scope of your research. This organizes your research and saves much time when writing the Memorial.

II. Characteristics of the Legal Research Paper

Unlike your argumentative Memorials, the research paper is intended to act as a guide to you and your teammates in structuring your arguments. There are, therefore, several important characteristics of a legal research paper.

A. *Argue both sides*

A legal research paper explains the law governing the issues. The writing is objective, not persuasive. The aim is to present to the reader the strongest arguments for both sides, not to persuade the reader to take sides by making strong arguments for one side and rebutting the other. Similarly, the legal research paper indicates the weaknesses of each argument. In short, writing a research paper will explain how the law is likely to be applied by the Court. The style of writing is similar to that you use when asked to take the role of a judge or to solve a problem during an exam.

B. *Point out imbalances and conflicts*

The law might favor one side. The sources for the claims might give tremendous support for one side and little or none for the other. The imbalance can be due to the lack of sufficient formal sources for the one side; in this case, the other side will likely rely on "soft law" or formal sources of law that are in the process of development. To give the reader an accurate understanding of how the law most likely will be applied, point out the imbalances and the conflicts.

Remember that there are always two sides to an argument, and the research paper should present weaker or alternative arguments in support of a stronger argument. Especially during oral arguments, when the judges or your opponents may present a surprising counter-argument, arguments that involve considerations of justice and policy can end up being quite important. (For a presentation on how to identify the latter two types of arguments, see Chapter 5, Section III.F and III.G).

Sources may also conflict. When explaining the authorities supporting the claims, point out those that are not in agreement. General principles of legal reasoning state that conflict between authorities is only apparent, and may be resolved with proper evaluation. Determine the weight of the sources and to what degree they are binding upon the parties. If your sources are cases, show how the facts of the cases compare, drawing analogies between some facts and distinguishing others.

III. Components of a Legal Research Paper

A. Heading

Begin your research paper with identifying the audience for which it is written, the author, the date and the subject.

B. Question Presented

List the legal question(s) addressed in the research paper arising from the facts of the case. (This is especially important for teams that divide the research among several team members, since it will allow the team to quickly distinguish among the research papers.) The "Questions Presented" should be listed in the same order as the legal issues are addressed in the research paper.

The preliminary research paper will concern the area of law that governs the claims. Early research papers will cover these areas broadly; later in the process, you may write shorter research papers concerning subsidiary issues or alternative legal arguments.

At this point, you will probably not be able to draft the precise Questions Presented until you have written the main "Discussion" section (see below, subsection D). Once you have completed the Discussion section of the paper, review and re-formulate the questions so that they that clearly present the specific legal questions that your Discussion addresses. Usually, one to three questions will suffice.

C. Applicable sources of international law

Although this comes before your Discussion section, you probably want to write this after that section is written. List the body of law—the treaties, case law, treatises and articles—that is relevant to discussing the Questions Presented. In this section, you need to include all of the sources that apply to your issue, not merely the sources that are necessary resolve the questions. Cite the proper titles of treaties or the cases where principles may be found. Also, you may wish to describe briefly the degree to which the sources are accepted as international law, and how the sources might be binding—or might be argued to be binding—upon the parties in your case. (See Chapter 8 for how to properly cite sources.)

D. *Discussion Section*

1. Six points on effective writing for the Discussion Section

To structure your discussion, consider the following points:

(i) *Headings.* Use separate headings for each issue according to your number of Questions Presented. Make sure the headings correspond to the content of the text below it. When one of the Questions Presented is complex, use sub-headings to break down the analysis. Depending on the nature of the issue, you can organize the discussion of an issue according to the sources of law, or according to the positions of the two parties.

(ii) *Paragraphs.* Organize your discussion into paragraphs logically. The first sentence of your paragraph should introduce the rest of the paragraph. The last sentence should conclude the content of the paragraph.

(iii) *Within the paragraph, let no legal statement stand alone.* In the text itself, distinguish clearly between legal and factual statements. Every legal statement or conclusion must be drawn from an acceptable source of international law; identify each of these sources with a footnote. This is very important at this stage of the process, since sentences making legal arguments without citation are not appropriate. With proper citations, therefore, the research paper will serve as a foundation for writing and footnoting the Memorial. This practice will save time, since you need the correct citation to be able to rely upon your research as accurate and accountable.

(iv) *Policy arguments.* The text may also contain arguments based upon of public policy, the needs of a state or the goals of the international legal system. Policy arguments are not necessarily extra-legal arguments because the policies argued may conceivably be found within or argued from the text of the law.

(v) *Non-substantive legal arguments.* The Court will decide the case at hand on the basis of the rules and principles of international law. However, the Court is also concerned with administering the international law in a just manner. Therefore, arguments of equity and proportionality contribute to making the international law a viable legal system.

(vi) *Matters of opinion.* It is very important to distinguish clearly between authoritative statements of law and matters of your own interpretation. All arguments that are not qualified with a footnote showing an acceptable source of international law should be regarded as personal assertions with limited legal importance.

2.   How to approach the writing

As in all legal writing, clarity and simplicity are required. Explain concepts clearly. Keep sentences short. Do not assume the reader knows anything about the specific area of law that governs your claims. However, you should assume that your readers (you and your teammates) have a grasp of basic concepts of international law.

Consider the following:

(i)   *Start with the background of the law.* Give a concise introduction to the subject. Do not assume that your reader knows the area of law you are researching. Present the main rules governing the area of law, and comment on how the rules are binding upon the parties. Point out what comes within the ambit of the treaties, the customary rules, and the general principles governing the area of law.

Describe the characteristics of the rules. Have the rules recently come into use? Are they disputed? What parts are not disputed? Which aspects of the rules cause problems to the application in international relations? Tie the introduction to the facts of your case.

(ii)   *Present the rules governing the issue.* Present the main rule. What requirements must be met in order for an action to be legal or illegal? Narrow down the area of law governing the issue, by pointing out the aspects of the rules that are silent if applied to your case. If several sources of law govern the area of law you are researching, analyze one source at the time. As you have analyzed all your different sources, synthesize them. Which are conflicting? Which support or complement each other?

(iii) *Connect to events in international affairs.* Events in international affairs can demonstrate how legal questions have been solved in the past. For instance, although a rule may be codified in a widely accepted treaty, do you know how many states are actually acting upon it?

(iv) *Consider non-substantive arguments and policy arguments.* During your analysis of the facts and your research you have probably gathered several arguments based on considerations of justice or on the policy of states. Include such arguments in order to get a sense of how the law might be applied.

E. Conclusion

The Conclusion section should briefly summarize the answers the Discussion section provides. The Conclusion should indicate the likelihood of either party succeeding. Also include a very short explanation of the grounds on which the questions are answered. Do not cite articles or cases, but summarize the body of the law.

F. Scope of research

During your trips to the library, you have probably read, browsed or studied more books, journals and other documents than is reflected in the Discussion section. Some of the sources and some of the search words might not have produced results. List the search words you used and the sources you consulted. Knowing what you have done may allow the reader to suggest other avenues.

CHAPTER 4

Preliminary Research

I.   Researching International Law

A.   *Some characteristics*

Research in international law is different than research in domestic law. In domestic law, the most important sources—statutes and decisions of certain courts—are systematically documented. At the international level, treaties are registered at the United Nations Treaty Series, and all cases from the International Court of Justice can be found in reporters. However, most other sources of international law, such as the state practice that forms the basis for international custom and general principles of law, are not systemized. In fact, most international custom and general principles have never been distilled into authoritative written rules.

There are, however, similarities between research in domestic and international law. Both domestic and international law contain vast undeveloped areas of law, where you will need to exercise some creativity as a researcher and writer. Furthermore, all legal research is inherently disorganized, imprecise and rife with dead-ends. The purpose of this Chapter is to reduce these frustrating traits of legal research, by providing steps that will point you directly to the relevant sources.

B. The object of the preliminary research

The main focus of the preliminary research is to identify the legal issues and the sub-issues arising from the claims. Identifying the issues involves getting an overview of the area of law in question. Remember that you need to identify the legal issues for both the applicant's and the respondent's claims, if they are different.

To ensure effective research, keep a copy of the Compromis with you at all times. The key to an effective argument will be your ability to relate the legal arguments to the specific factual situations. Which research approach you use (see Chapter 2, Section IV) is not important; in all likelihood, you will use several different methods interchangeably.

Orderly research will serve you well when writing the Memorial. For this reason, keep a log of all the research steps you make. The research log will document which avenues you have explored, listing books, treaties and sources you have read and search words and databases you have utilized.

In the following example of a research log, a five-step approach for the preliminary research is presented. At the end of Chapter 5, a library reference list is provided.

RESEARCH LOG: *The Football League Case*

Research Tools Type	Search words	Document	Hits	Date Searched
International Law Dictionary	Self-determination		1	Sep.9.99
UN Treaty Series Search	Self-determination	Original agreement	26	Sep.9.99
The World Court Digest	Use of force	Merits	34	Sep.9.99

The first column, "Research Tools," is simply a list of different sources you have used in conducting your research. The second column, "Search Words," lists any key words you used in each resource to identify likely materials. The third column, "Type of document," lists the kind of source the research tool includes. The fourth column, "Hits," is simply a count of the number of occurrences of your search words within the research tool. The final column, "Date Searched," indicates the last time you searched this particular research tool.

II. Compiling a Source Book

A "source book" is a list of sources of international law. The source book will include copies of all of the treaties that are directly relevant to the issues you have identified.

Begin your source book by identifying the relevant treaties that the states are party to. These are listed near the end of the Compromis. Print or make a copy of the full text of the treaties. Make sure also to note how many and what other states are party to the convention, and when the treaty entered into force. The full-text of most treaties can be found in the any of several volumes by publishing houses that publish material collections of basic documents in international law (see list of recommended reading at the end of Chapter 5). There are also material collections on specific subject matters, like Human Rights, Environmental Law or International Economic Law. If you cannot find the treaty printed in any of these compilations, consult the United Nations Treaty Series, which includes most treaties deposited with the United Nations Secretary-General.

The most important international instruments should also be included in your sourcebook: these include, at the very least, the Statute of the International Court of Justice, the United Nations Charter, the Vienna Convention on the Law of Treaties (the "VCLT"), and the Universal Declaration of Human Rights. Depending on the subject-matter of the Compromis, you may also wish to include one or more of the General Assembly's Friendly Relations Declaration, the International Covenant on Civil and Political Rights, and/or the International Covenant on Economic, Social and Cultural Rights.

Keep these documents in a folder with a copy of the Compromis. Consider the folder as the most important document in your research process.

III. Defining the Areas of Law

A. *Analyze the claims in the Compromis*

The areas of law that govern a given issue can be determined by an analysis of the claims. Usually the area of law is directly stated, and your previous knowledge of how domestic law is organized will in most instances apply in international law as well.

For instance, one party may request the Court to declare that the acts of the other party constitute expropriation. Drawing on your previous knowledge of law, the claim is identified as an issue of expropriation and falls under economic or property law. The party may then request the Court to declare that some adoptions of children evacuated from an emergency situation is not inconsistent with international law. The claim may be identified as an issue of children's rights, and falls under Human Rights.

In some cases, the claim may not readily fall into a substantive area of law, but may be identified in some other way. For example, the Court is asked to compel one party to deliver to the other party all copies of a database, and refrain from making any use whatsoever of the materials contained therein. This claim may not readily be identified if you rely merely upon your previous substantive knowledge of international law. However, looking at the nature of the relief itself, you should be able to identify it as a request for injunctive relief in the form of an order. Another remedy frequently requested is reparations in the form of monetary damages, by asking the Court to award damages for injuries suffered.

B. Identify other relevant issues

Sometimes all the issues are not explicitly mentioned. Identifying all relevant issues requires consideration of issues that may arise from the facts. For example:

- One issue may give rise to several obligations. If the claim concerns the adoption of unaccompanied children, both the state of origin and the adopting state may have obligations toward the children, the adopting state may have obligations towards the state of origin, and the state of origin may have rights as a sovereign state.
- Some issues may call for a discussion of the Court's competence or other questions concerning its jurisdiction. For instance, the Court may or may not have competence to rule on questions arising from the instruments of the World Trade Organization (WTO), if the organs of the WTO have reserved exclusive authority to interpret the agreement. Similar situations may arise in any fact-pattern where a separate competent body has reserved jurisdiction over a treaty or a legal regime.
- Other issues may require a discussion of standing of the parties. The point of departure is that there must be a link recognized under international law between a nation and a claim for relief. The nature and

extent of a recognized link is often a hotly-debated point before moot court judges.
- An issue concerning the appropriate use of a rule (or of exceptions to the rule) may require an extensive discussion.
- Specific remedies frequently require a discussion as to whether the Court can issue the kind of relief asked for.

C. Familiarize yourself with the topic

When you have determined the correct topic, read a comprehensive summary of the topic under in a legal encyclopedia (see list of recommended reading at the end of Chapter 5). The summary will explain and define your topic, and may serve as the introduction to the Discussion section in your initial research paper. Note the meaning of particular terms, any summary of important documents or cases, and any further references the encyclopedia may have.

Compare the summary in the encyclopedia with an introductory textbook on international law. Note where opinions diverge, or if the textbook provides any new references.

Remember however, that an encyclopedia is in most cases not an appropriate source of authority in international law. For this reason, you cannot in most cases refer to a mere encyclopedia article in your Memorial. An exception occurs when the author is particularly well-known and respected in his field; for this reason, take down the name of the author of the entry and make a note to investigate his standing in the field.

IV. Defining the Main Rules, Conditions and Exceptions

A. Where are rules stated?

Now it is time to determine the content of the rules governing the area of law that the claims concern. Keep the source book with the Compromis nearby in order to ensure that you are connecting the research of the topic to the facts of the case.

Consult an introductory textbook on international law to find which rules govern the issue. In some cases, introductory books do not cover your topic, in which case, you will need to find an alternate basic source for your topic.

In order to find a textbook or journal that can introduce you to the main legal points, search a library or Internet database for books on your topic. Select a book or volume on the topic, preferably a recent publication. Read the summary to determine if the text is relevant to the facts of your case. For example, if the claim in your case concerns the adoption of children, an appropriate volume would address the rights of unaccompanied children; a source that focuses on the child labor laws would not be relevant to the case.

If the volume is relevant, go to the table of contents to identify the relevant subtopics. A relevant source would refer to right of the unaccompanied child in the content of an emergency situation. If the table of contents reveals that the source only treats the right of the unaccompanied child under stabile conditions, the source is only of cursory interest to the case.

B. Identify the rules

When you have found and read the appropriate text, formulate the rules applied to the facts of your case. As in all legal work, a comprehensive understanding of the rules governing the areas of law includes the wordings of the main rules, its conditions and the exceptions.

For instance, if the topic is on expropriation, the main rule is that expropriation may be executed in international law. Three conditions must be met for a legal expropriation:: the expropriation must have a public purpose, it must be non-discriminatory and full compensation must be given. For each of the conditions there may be exceptions depending on the circumstances of the case.

V. Analyzing the Kind of Sources the Rule Is Based Upon

Identify which source the rules rest upon by referring to article 38(1) of the Statute of the Court. Determine whether the grounds for the rules are international conventions, international custom, general principles of law, or subsidiary means of determining rules of law. Not all sources fit neatly into the list provided in article 38(1) of the Statute of the Court. For instance, special issues regarding the binding authority of resolutions of international organizations may arise. Particular consideration may be applied if custom and treaties overlap. As in domestic law, the basis for the rule can also be found in arguments based on policy and in non-substantive legal arguments. Furthermore, if the ground is a principle developed by an International Court, be sure to note which court delivered the judgment, and the specifics of the case. (Only if the text offers this information, as you are not supposed to do in-depth research at this stage. If not, make a note of these points for your advanced research.)

VI. Evaluating the Claims Made

The last task before writing the initial research paper is to evaluate the claims made. This accomplishes two things: You will remind yourself on the mutual dependence between the facts and the law, and you will ascertain problem areas relevant to your advanced research. The rounding off of your initial research will also start the first steps of your advanced research.

A. *Connect the rules to the facts*

Start with connecting the rules to the facts. Does the state making the claim have any factual basis for making the claim? Is the factual basis uncertain? Evaluate the strength of each claim when connected to the facts.

For instance, if one state seeks an order of the Court to award remedies for injuries suffered, a review of the Compromis may show that it is difficult to determine the actual loss. In another instance, a state that seeks an order of the Court to declare discrimination of foreigners inconsistent with international law may be more likely to win its claim if the Compromis shows that foreigners are discriminated in effect as well as in law.

B. *Evaluate the body of law*

As earlier discussed, determining the strength of each claim requires identifying imbalances and conflicts in the body of law. Since international law is a system which is both flexible and in many respects inconclusive, you have a great responsibility as a researcher and advocate to make conclusions as to how the Court is most likely to apply the law.

1. The apparently weak claims

Identify the claims that have no or little support in sources that are binding upon the parties. Identify possibilities for strengthening the claim.

For instance, if there is a treaty that is directly relevant, but only one party has ratified the treaty, while the other has merely signed it, the treaty can only be applied to the extent which the signatory state is bound. In other instances, the only source supporting an argument may be the teachings of a highly qualified publicist. If the authoritative sources are lacking, the argument will most likely be based on policy and non-substantive legal arguments.

2. The apparently strong claims

All arguments have a weak link. One state may be favored with sources that authoritatively are both specific and binding. Carefully examine each parts of the legal argument that constitutes the seemingly well-supported rule to find the trouble spot. Then identify the approach that will serve as the linchpins of the claim.

For instance, if a state's claim concerns terrorism, the sources supporting the claim that terrorism is illegal are well documented in international law. The trouble spot would most likely be to define terrorism. The linchpin to the argument is the ability of the state to point to a definition of terrorism grounded in an authoritative source under article 38(1) of the Statute of the Court.

3. Claims that can be supported and refuted with equal strength

Some claims may have authoritative sources that both support and reject the claim. If sources conflict, try to determine the outcomes of the supporting and the opposing arguments. As in domestic law, treaties, customs, and principles operate within a certain ambit.

For instance, discrimination in trade on the basis of nationality does not constitute a violation of customary international law. Therefore, it is most likely a matter of the sovereign power of states. However, a multitude of bilateral treaties gives rise to an obligation to observe national treatment. These bilateral treaties can be used as evidence of customary international law. The principle of sovereign equality must be balanced against a possible customary obligation. Point out how the sources can be synthesized.

CHAPTER 5

Advanced Research

I.   The Object of the Advanced Research

The next phase of your preparation will be "advanced research," in which you delve in detail into the legal issues specifically raised in the Compromis. In the advanced research each member of your team must focus on the claims for the side he or she will represent. While the initial research essentially requires you to explain the law applied to the facts, the object of the advanced research is to look for specific solutions to the claims. You will now resolve the conflicts and the imbalance problems you identified when evaluating the initial research (Chapter 3.VI).

Some of the claims are easier to support than others. As a lawyer representing your client, you must find convincing arguments for the difficult claims as well. Where legal sources are wholly lacking, you must propose new rules yourself, the way courts do when confronted with a factual situation that has no obvious answer. This task may require some creativity, combined with an understanding of how reasonable legal arguments can be derived from the different sources of international law. Your challenge is to develop a notion of when it is possible to seek an equitable solution, on the one hand, and when the strict rule of law must be accepted, on the other.

II. Approaching the Advanced Research

At this stage, it is inevitable that you will encounter some dead-ends in your research. The approach presented in the following cannot alleviate all the frustrations of the process. Keep in mind, however, that the Compromis is designed to present problems that do not have one definite solution. Again, the key to finding effective arguments in your research will depend on your ability to relate the legal authorities to the facts.

The overall goal of the advanced research is to find the proper material that supports your case. In the first instance, this is a matter of distinguishing between useful references and less useful references. For this, a research strategy is needed (See Part III of this Chapter, below). Advanced research is also a matter of properly identifying a rule of law that may be applied to the facts of your case. This identification requires knowledge of how to construe and apply the sources of international law (See Part IV of this Chapter, below). The rules derived from the sources must be tested against the general or fundamental principles of international law. In this phase, you may find it useful to refer to Part V, which contains a brief summary of some of the most important principles of international law. You must also develop a full argument by addressing the policy questions and explain the fairness of your position (See Part VI of this Chapter). Finally, you must consider the extent to which the Court may choose between a restrictive or an activist course in the case (See Part VII of this Chapter).

Note that when finding arguments to support your position during research, take care to support each legal statement with a citation, in order to save time when converting your research into a formal Memorial.

At the end of this Chapter is a bibliography of basic library references you may find useful in your advanced research.

III. Research Strategy—Advanced Research

The following research strategy involves a three-step procedure. In addition to these three steps, you will need to know when to stop, as legal research is by its very nature indefinite.

A. *Start with the sources that provide the strongest possible argument*

Article 38(1) of the Statute of the International Court of Justice sets forth five categories of legal sources upon which the International Court of

Justice must base its judgments. The first three sources enumerated in Article 38(1) are as follows:

a.   International conventions, whether general or particular, establishing rules expressly recognized by the contesting parties,
b.   International custom, as evidence of a general practice accepted as law
c.   General principles of law recognized by the civilized nations.

These are considered the most important sources of international law because they are sources the Court may always take into consideration. Although the Statute does not establish the relative importance of the three sources, many experts believe that the article indicates a reasonable ranking of the sources. For the purposes of international law moot court, the order of the sources in the article gives the recommended order for research. Therefore, start the advanced research by examining possibly relevant treaties, and continue with sources that express customary law and general principles.

The other two sources listed in Article 38 are contained in Section (d), and are:

d.   Judicial decisions and the teachings of the most highly qualified publicists.

These two sources are not law per se, but are, according to Article 38, the "subsidiary means for the determination of rules of law." They become very important in helping to focus the research process. Writings of scholars are particularly useful both as research aids and as sources of law. In most instances, they collect and preserve international principles derived from the other three sources.

B.   *Expand by drawing analogies or distinguish the case*

International law is not a fully developed body of law, and you must sometimes use principles from another area of law. This will require you to draw analogies between an unresolved legal question arising under international law and an answer arising under a different body of law. When drawing analogies, determine the extent of the principle, how it can be binding, and if multiple principles exist which to apply to your case.

For instance, in the *Corfu Channel Case*, the Court stated that a state has a duty under international law to prevent any activity that causes damage to another state. In addition to the original context of the rule, jurists have frequently cited this principle in the context of trans-boundary environmental injury, and it can also effectively be extended to other areas of law, such as state responsibility for terrorism.

C. Settle on policy arguments and non-substantial legal arguments

When the applicable sources are analyzed and possible analogies have been drawn, conclude your research with the third category of arguments: policy arguments and considerations of justice. Policy arguments explain the "whys" of the rule, and the beneficial outcome of applying a rule in the case on hand, and are necessary parts of any argument in international law. Non-substantive legal arguments determine that the conclusion favoring your party is a just one, and is essential in international law, a legal system that requires no prior explicit consent from the parties.

D. When to stop

When to end the research is a decision which relies in part upon your own personal ambition. But even the most ambitious researchers are confined by deadlines, as well as the fact that circumstances continuously change and new sources are constantly added to the picture. Research is by its nature indefinite. But regardless of the level of ambition, the research must show certain characteristics before it can be regarded as completed.

Be certain that you base your arguments on all the working treaties that govern the issue. Your research on customary law must be representative (universal) and give some evaluation of whether there is *opinio juris*. All general principles of international law in relevant writings of jurists and judicial decisions must have been discussed. Considerations of justice and policy arguments should be derived from all sources applied.

E. Still facing unresolved questions?

Extended research cannot wipe out all residue of doubt as to the quality of your position. At least some aspects of the case will remain nebulous. This aspect of uncertainty requires the judge to make a choice between possible norms of international law. The principle governing the judge's choice is the question of whether the Court should apply a restrictive or an expansive approach to international law: that is, whether the judge wishes to conservatively rely upon well-established rules or to develop new rules. You must strengthen your position by identifying in which issues you wish the court to be restrictive or activist, and then by appealing to the duty and role of the Court in limiting and developing international law.

IV. How to Construe and Apply the Sources of International Law Listed in Article 38(I)

A. *International Conventions and Treaties*

In the preliminary research, the first treaties you researched were found by evaluating the issues raised in the Compromis. You found additional treaties by consulting the writings of jurists which usually refer to all important treaties or conventions related to the issue.

In advanced research, you must conduct a more sophisticated search for applicable treaties. Whenever dealing with treaties, you must make sure to note whether a treaty has entered into force, which and how many states have ratified the treaty, and which and how many states have merely signed the treaty.

1. Find all applicable treaties that govern your issue

The object of advanced treaty research is to confirm whether a treaty that is binding between the parties has provisions that govern your issue. In addition to collecting all treaties that directly govern an issue, this step also requires that you re-analyze the issue for the purpose of finding new areas of law by which the issue may be governed. For example, copyright is normally thought of as part of private international law. However, referring to Article 27 in the Universal Declaration of Human Rights, some jurists have argued that copyright is also a subset of human rights law. Thus, you may argue that copyright law is also governed by human rights law, and may make reference to human-rights treaties in a case concerning copyright.

2. Interpret the treaty

Advanced research requires a close interpretation of the applicable treaties. First, find out if there are books or articles that specifically discuss the treaty in question. Second, review relevant provisions in the VCLT, the international instrument that discusses generally the rules regarding treaty interpretation. You may also wish to refer to a general book that discusses the interpretation and application of treaties to remind yourself of the basic principles. In addition, the intention of the parties to a treaty may also be discovered by looking at the historical context and at the records of the negotiations. For the historical context, consult the preparatory work. The records of the negotiations are called the *travaux preparatoires* and can be regarded, according to the Vienna Convention, as a subsidiary means of interpretation in international law.

3.   Research on the United Nations Charter

Practically all states—and nearly all fictional states in international law moot court problems—are members of the United Nations. Therefore provisions of the Charter of the United Nations are very important. However, the Charter does not contain many principles which create definite legal obligations. Therefore, be careful not to jump to conclusions when applying the Charter. Consult one of the many books written on the Charter for guidance on this problem.

B. *Custom*

It is important that you understand what customary international law is and is not, before attempting to use it in international law. For a thorough discussion of the elements and philosophy of the concept of customary international law, you should consult a more exhaustive treatment in a textbook on public international law.

Customary international law is an important source of international law, as all states are bound by it, regardless of prior consent. Custom is also an extremely important source in international law moot court, since the thorny problems that form the basis for most moot court problems are usually solved by reference to custom. Unfortunately, it is very difficult to prove that a particular proposition has developed into a norm of customary international law.

In order to prove that a particular proposition has become customary international law, you must demonstrate that the proposition satisfies both necessary elements: (1) consistent state practice and (2) *opinio juris*. It is nearly impossible for a moot court participant to prove the state practice to the degree that would be required in actual practice of law. Therefore, in international law moot court, you should employ a "shortcut" method to find "evidence" of customary international law.

1.   Multilateral and bilateral treaties

Customary international law may be articulated in multilateral or bilateral agreements. If the requirements of customary international law are met, a principle of law can be embodied in a number of multilateral or bilateral agreements. For example, it is difficult to show the *opinio juris* for the principle of "national treatment" in international trade law. However, it can be argued that *opinio juris* can be proved from the fact that the principle is expressed in GATT, which has 145 parties, and the more than 300 bilateral treaties that apply the same principle. You can find support for this type of argument by consulting the research sources on conventions and treaties discussed above. To focus your research, keep the following points in mind:

(i)   *Is the principle uniform?* The most important point in custom resulting from treaties is to determine whether that principle has universal or general recognition. In other words, if two treaties use the same term ("national treatment"), but use it to mean two fundamentally different concepts, you cannot use both treaties in support of the same principle. It is not necessary to show the absolute general practice; substantial uniformity is sufficient.

(ii)   *Is the principle representative?* If the dispute is between a developing and a developed state, the researcher must show that the principle is "custom" with respect to both developed and developing states. A so-called "custom" which has only received acceptance in documents of Western European and North American states, for example, may not actually be representative of the state practice and intent of all states. In international trade law example, both the GATT and the numerous bilateral agreements discussed have a considerable number of parties from both developing and developed states. That is a positive point to argue for customary international law.

(iii)   *What part of the treaty can prove customary international law?* It is not necessary to show that the entire treaty, including each individual provision, has become customary international law. You need only prove that the particular provision addressing the issue raised in the Compromis has become custom. A common example in this respect is the Universal Declaration on Human Rights, which contains many provisions that have become custom, and many other provisions that have not.

(iv) *How long has the principle been practiced?* Consider whether the treaty is new or old. It is difficult to argue that provisions first expressed in a new treaty have crystallized into customary law. For example, in the case of copyright, TRIPS is a very recent treaty and it is difficult to show that the convention is customary law. Keep in mind, however, that sometimes a relatively new treaty may simply restate or codify existing customary law, as is the case for certain provisions in the UN Convention on the Law of the Sea ("UNCLOS").

2. Actions taken by states thorough international organizations

Actions taken by States thorough international organizations, such as Resolutions, declarations and statements of principle of the United Nations General Assembly may also be evidence of state practice or *opinio juris*. States adopt certain rules through international organizations, and it may be argued that States will follow these statements in practice. This is especially true of Resolutions and the like which have been approved by the General Assembly by a wide margin.

General Assembly Resolutions are particularly significant in international law. For example, when arguing that customary international law requires that a valid state expropriation must have a public purpose, you might rely on the fact that this principle has repeatedly been affirmed in several General Assembly Resolutions, and then list the Resolutions. Information on General Assembly Resolutions can be obtained by consulting a textbook, or by searching the United Nations record for General Assembly resolutions.

The Yearbook of International Law Commission (ILC) is also an important source to determine state practice or *opinio juris*. The ILC Yearbook is published annually in two volumes, and records the activities of the International Law Commission, the United Nations commission of specialists charged with development of international law. Over the years, the ILC has drafted, debated, and adopted a number of proposed treaties, many of which codify customary law.

National yearbooks of international law are also an important source of information about the practice of states. These yearbooks, which are essentially summaries of international law as practiced within a particular state, frequently reprint domestic court decisions that apply or interpret international law. In addition, some contain summaries of new legislation or brief descriptions of executive actions.

3. Decisions of international tribunals

The reasoning and justification of the judgments of international tribunals, particularly the decisions of the Permanent Court of International Justice (PCIJ) (the predecessor court to the ICJ) and the ICJ, are also frequently offered as evidence of customary law. As the ICJ Statute itself states, judicial decisions are taken as subsidiary means of finding the law. In its judgments, the ICJ will frequently engage in a lengthy analysis of whether a given principle is a customary norm. If this reasoning supports your argument, you can use the reasoning of the Court to support your position. For example, in the *Case Concerning Military and Paramilitary Activities in and against Nicaragua (Nicar. v. U.S.)* (1986) (the "Nicaragua Case"), the ICJ discussed and then affirmed that the principle of non-intervention is a tenet of customary international law. The existence of a decision can be gathered from the writings of the publicists, from the ICJ's (or other tribunal's) website, or by consulting published summaries of ICJ decisions.

4. National decisions and national legislation following a particular rule of law

National decisions and national legislation can also constitute evidence of state practice. Such "municipal" law has limited strength as evidence of customary international law, especially if you apply it as your primary evidence of customary status. However, a list of national decisions and legislation in support of your principle can be a powerful supporting argument for a rule of customary international law.

In order to find domestic caselaw, follow the guidelines discussed in Section D below. As for national legislation, the most efficient method of gathering different national legislation on a particular matter is to consult an article or book that focuses on the subject.

5. Diplomatic correspondence and administrative decision can be evidence of custom

Diplomatic correspondence and administrative decisions can also be evidence of state practice and *opinio juris*. If the issue concerns only a handful of states, it is not an insurmountable research task to gather representative statements; one likely source is local Embassies. However, be aware that state practice is more extensive than mere diplomatic correspondence

7. Counter research that the particular norm is not customary law

Proving that a given norm is not customary international law is easier than proving that such norm is customary international law. Although there are no distinct guidelines as to how to demonstrate that a particular norm is not customary law, you may think of this process as simply a matter of demonstrating that your opponent cannot prove his position by use of any of the methods listed in the previous section. In particular, look for the following to show a particular norm is not customary law:

(i) *The persistent objector rule.* If a state has persistently objected to the customary-law status of a given tenet, then under certain circumstances the tenet does not become custom with respect to that state. The Compromis may show that the researcher's state may be a persistent objector to a given customary norm. For a closer treatment of the requirements of the persistent objector rule, consult *Anglo-Norwegian Fisheries Case*, 1951 ICJ 116.

(ii) *Lack of clear or subsequent state practice.* If a principle in a treaty is not stated clearly, or if there is no subsequent uniform state practice consistent with that principle, this is strong evidence that the principle does not in fact constitute customary international law. For example, one of the reasons why the ICJ in the *North-Sea Continental Shelf Case*, stated that "the equidistant principle" as mentioned in North Sea Continental Conventions is not a customary norm was that the principle itself was not clear and subsequent state practice was not uniform. In this respect, also consider whether the treaty is so recent that there is insufficient time to determine whether subsequent state practice is consistent.

(iii) *Reservations during the negotiations of the treaty.* Examine the views of the states' representatives during the formulation of the treaty.

If there was disagreement among the states during negotiations, then non-parties might argue that there is no strong consensus, and therefore the principle is not customary law. For example, during the formation of the TRIPS agreement, the developing countries consistently objected to the standard of protection for intellectual property proposed by the developed states, and these disputes continued long after the negotiations concluded.

(iv) *Conflicting judicial decisions.* In a given case, different justices may disagree as to the customary status of a given principle. Justices who dissent from the establishment of a given norm will provide support for their positions, and you can use the evidence they produce as evidence against the norm. For example, in *the Advisory Opinion on the legality on the Use or Threat of Nuclear Weapons* the ICJ was divided on the point of establishing several principles as customary international law.

(v) *Conflicting theory.* Much like the ICJ justices just discussed, leading writers may frequently disagree as to the status of law. You can use their research in the same fashion. Determine different views by comparing the texts, or by examining the footnotes or endnotes in books or articles.

C. General Principles

"General principles of law recognized by civilized nations" is the third primary source mentioned in the ICJ Statute. The scope of the application of these general principles is not yet determined in international law. The following important points should be mentioned to clarify the position of the source:

This source of international law authorizes the ICJ to apply general principles of municipal jurisprudence, in particular of private law, in so far as they are applicable relations among states. But this does not mean that the ICJ should automatically borrow all the principles recognized by the civilized legal systems.

The ICJ has resorted to general principles to establish international law relating to evidence, procedure, and damages. The Court may also use general principles to support any substantive body of law that has been influenced historically and logically by domestic law. In addition, the Court will employ elements of legal reasoning, non-substantial legal arguments, and private law analogies in order to make international legal system a viable system for application in a judicial process.

D. *Judicial Decisions*

Judicial decisions, a subsidiary source of international law, include decisions from international and national tribunals and from arbitrating bodies. These decisions are sources of international law because they establish and record that law. The focus of the research of judicial decision is to determine which principles can be derived from the decisions. If a particular case is important to the research, then it may be appropriate to read the whole case or parts of the case from its actual reports.

The most helpful tool to interpret judicial decisions is casebooks, textbooks and articles. Casebooks provide a discussion of important cases by topic. Textbooks and articles usually have references to a greater variety of cases, but do not give a closer discussion of the strengths and weaknesses of each case.

When searching for established principles derived from judicial decisions, note that the principles may not be explicitly stated. Before ending your research, you should make sure to consult the actual text of the decision to be able to provide accurate page and paragraph reference where the court stated the law.

1.   Decisions from international tribunals

There are many international tribunals at work. Some international tribunals only resolve claims arising from specific historical events and are not permanent in nature (*e.g.* the Iran-United States Claims Tribunal or the International Criminal Tribunal for the Former Yugoslavia). Others limit their jurisdiction to conflicts arising under specific international conventions. The most important tribunals applying general international law are:

*   The International Court of Justice
*   The Permanent Court of International Justice
*   The International Criminal Court
*   The Permanent Court of Arbitration
*   The European Court of Human Rights
*   The Inter-American Court of Human Rights
*   The International Center for the Settlement of Investment Disputes

- Decisions from the WTO Judicial Body
- The Court of Justice of the European Union

2. Decisions from national courts

Decisions of national courts are significant only to the extent that they are (a) determining an issue of international law or (b) indications of "general principles of law."

E. Teachings of the Publicist

Although in actual practice this also is a subsidiary source, in international law moot court, it is an important source of international law. Books and articles evaluate and discuss treaties, customs, general principles of law, and judicial decisions. Do not assume that statements in books are of more significance than statements in articles. Books contain longer, in-depth discussions and presentations of issues of law. But thorough research usually consists of finding a considerable number of articles on a particular subject. Consider that articles as well as books evaluate the law, provide critical studies and also refer to other views. In addition, articles provide shorter, in-depth discussions on a particular topic, and therefore are useful for the researcher working under a deadline. You can find relevant articles in journals by consulting footnotes in books or other articles, in various online and electronic databases, or simply by reading the table of contents of a likely journal. (If using the table-of-contents method, begin with the most recent volume, and work backwards. The advantage of starting with the latest one is that it will provide cites to previously published articles.)

The opinions of the scholars differ for many reasons, including their national origin and political or philosophical position. Read books and articles from writers having different backgrounds. For similar reasons, you should consult different journals published in different countries. The titles may be found by searching the database, or by simply browsing the library shelves by topic.

Authors disagree. This is important to keep in mind when you have difficulty finding any author supporting your position, or difficulty reconciling conflicting statements. Examine the footnotes of an author who takes a position contrary to your argument. The sources the author uses may be interpreted in a different way. The author may also have kindly included a reference to an opposing view, and how they might be reconciled.

V. Principles of International Law

International law is made up of certain principles that are thought to be of importance for the functioning of the international legal system. In reading textbooks on international law, you may have seen these principles referred to as "general principles of international law," or even "fundamental principles of international law." The agreement of your position with these general principles of international law can prove to be strong support of your proposed rule.

To develop a comprehensive argument, test the arguments you have developed based upon the traditional sources of international law (discussed in the preceding section) against the available principles of international law. Principles of international law may be difficult to identify, especially if you are unfamiliar with the concept of arguing on the basis of principles.

In this section, we discuss the use of these general principles in an argument, beginning with some discussion of the function and status of general principles of international law (See Part A, below). In Parts B and C, some of the leading general principles are identified and discussed

A. Function and status of general principles of international law

1. The function of general principles of international law

The operation of principles of law may be second nature to students from legal systems based upon the Anglo-Saxon legal tradition. Students from other jurisdictions may regard the application of "general principles" as strange or unfamiliar.

Principles of international law constitute an integrating factor among disparate concepts, and exist to enhance coherence of and structure among the set of rules which constitute a legal order. Therefore, the strength of a principle is measured by the degree to which it promotes such coherence and structure.

To apply a principle of international law, observe the following steps:

(i) Start by elaborating the various levels at which the principle is to play its integrating role in the making of international law. It is not sufficient merely to refer to a principle as the deciding factor without a description of its particular parts.
(ii) Continue to balance the different elements and standards contained in the principles. Again, the mere reference to a balancing test or standard does not ensure the rightful application of principles.

Principles function properly when applied in circumstances comparable to those in which they were originally enunciated, and when applied consistently with their policy objectives.

(iii) Finally, consider the merit of the principle. The prior declaration or acceptance of a principle by an authority does not ensure its appropriateness in all cases. Some principles, for instance the "equity principle," are actually no more than a compendium of somewhat disparate principles. As a result, the application of principles requires an analysis of its relevance in the present case.

2.   The status of principles of international law as a source of law

Principles are regarded as a source of law, and may serve as the basis of a legal argument. Some of the general principles of international law are often treated as fundamentally important to the international legal system, while others have limited application. At the same time, the principles are frequently treated as a category of sources somewhat different from the primary sources in Article 38(a). The following points are apparent:

Fundamental or basic principles of law regulating social intercourse make up the necessary foundation of any legal system. The international legal system is no different.

(i)   The difference between fundamental and other leading principles of international law.

  • International law contains a set of fundamental principles that serves as the very foundation of the legal system. In national systems, the fundamental principles may be found in written constitutions. The basic principles of international law have their origins in part in the old Westphalia order, and have emerged in the trends evidenced with the formation of the United Nations system. The fundamental principles of international law are enshrined in the United Nations Charter and its authoritative interpretations, and in the General Assembly Resolution No. 2625 (XXV) (1970), the "Declaration on Principles of International Law concerning Friendly Relations and Co-operation among States in accordance with the Charter of the United Nations" (the "Friendly Relations Declaration"). Other sources of law may expand upon the principles stipulated in the Charter and the Friendly Relations Declaration. If you are successful in linking the content of a provision in a bilateral treaty to a fundamental principle, this will give great weight to your argument as the fundamental principles of international law are binding on all United Nations Member States and other international subjects.

- Other leading principles of international law may be identified in treaties, the practice of states and perhaps in the general principles derived from national law.

(ii) Principles of international law as binding upon states.

- Much like custom, principles are legal norms that do not require prior consent of the parties. They are assumed and need no prior consent to be binding upon states. In this sense their provenance is related to that to customary international law.

- Regardless of in what source you find the principle, a mere mentioning of principles of international law is unlikely to provide a satisfactory basis for decisions. Standing alone they tend to be too imprecise, and do not in themselves identify binding rights and obligations.

- However, even the most sweeping and indeterminate principles do not diminish their importance as sources of law. Grand principles are significant as concepts of law to ease the appropriate application of substantial norms in particular cases.

- In sum, there are no clear-cut conclusions to be drawn about the relative importance to your argument of a given principle of international law *vis-à-vis* the other sources of law enumerated in article 38(I). A principle generally held to be of fundamental importance may be too indeterminate to be of significance in your specific case. Meanwhile, a less-important principle may clearly define legal relationships. In this situation, the less-important principle may, in fact, be better for your case.

B. *Fundamental principles of international law*

The fundamental principles of international law can be roughly divided into two categories: substantive principles of international law and procedural principles of international law.

1. Substantive principles of international law

1. *The principle of "sovereign equality of states"*

The principle of sovereignty dates back to the Westphalian order, and is the most basic principle in international law. It derives from the Charter of the United Nations itself. Art. 2(1) of the Charter states, "The Organization is based on the principle of sovereign equality of all its members." This principle has two main aspects, internal and external. The internal aspect concerns a State's exclusive jurisdiction, *prima facie* (presumed to be true unless disproved), over its territory and the permanent population living there. The external aspect imposes a duty on all other States not to intervene in this area of exclusive domestic jurisdiction. Sovereignty, however, is not absolute. For example, in exercising its sovereign right, a State cannot act contrary to its international obligations. The concept of sovereignty does not mean that a State is above the law.

The many aspects of sovereignty are expressed in numerous cases before the international courts. For example, in the Nicaragua Case, the ICJ addressed the question of non-intervention with respect to sovereignty. In the *Case of the SS "Lotus"* (Fr. v. Turk.), PCIJ Series A, No. 10 (1927) (the "Lotus Case"), the Permanent Court of International Justice addressed the issue of exclusive jurisdiction in relation to sovereignty.

Source: Nicaragua Case, 1986 I.C.J. 14, at pp. 392–394; and the Lotus Case at 18.

2. *Self-determination of peoples*

The principles of self-determination relate, like the principle of sovereignty, to international subjects. Unlike the principle of sovereignty, self-determination reflects more recent trends emerging in the world community. Self-determination is a controversial principle, embedded in Article 1(2) and Article 56(2) of the United Nations Charter. The principle has been the subject of a large number of General Assembly Resolutions, notably the Declaration on the Granting of Independence to Colonial Countries and Peoples, Resolution No. 1514 (XV) (1960), and the resolution on Permanent Sovereignty over Natural Resources, Resolution No. 1803 (XVII) (1962). Self-determination is upheld in Article 1 of both the United Nations Covenant on Civil and Political Rights and the Covenant on Economic, Social and Cultural Rights. It is also enunciated in the Friendly Relations Declaration and in the First Protocol Additional to the four 1949 Geneva Conventions on War Victims in 1977. These instruments testify to the crystallization of a binding fundamental principle of international law. Some authors argue that the principle is a *jus cogens* norm, that is, a peremptory norm of international law. The principle of self-determination imposes obligations on states and rights *erga omnes*, that is, rights which are vested in the international community as a whole (rather than in one particular treaty partner).

Three rights and duties may be derived from the principle:

(i)   States are duty-bound to allow the free exercise of self-determination of its peoples; in particular, States are enjoined not to forcibly deny them the right to self-determination.
(ii) Peoples entitled to self-determination have legal rights in relation to States in which they reside, as well as a host of rights and claims in regard of other states.
(iii) Third-party States are duty-bound to support peoples entitled to self-determination. If self-determination is forcibly denied, third-party States may bring the question before the competent United Nations bodies and can resort to peaceful sanctions.

3.   Prohibition of the threat or use of force

The prohibition of the threat or use of force is enunciated in Article 2(4) of the UN Charter. This enunciation was a direct response to the horrors of the Second World War, and is now regarded as a fundamental principle of international law. The principle imposes both obligations and rights *erga omnes* and is thought of as non-derogable. The principle has the following main components:

(i)   The ban on force is an absolute all-inclusive prohibition, except in those circumstances provided for in Article 51 of the Charter. The Friendly Relations Declaration and the General Assembly's Resolution on the Definition of Aggression, G.A. Res. 3314 (XXIX) (1974) (the "Aggression Declaration") modifies the right of anticipatory self-defense.
(ii) Only military force is proscribed in the United Nations Charter. Non-military force—for example, "economic aggression" or transboundary environmental "aggression" is not covered in the Charter. The Friendly Relations Declaration and the Aggression Declaration also proscribe the use of economic force. But the aggrieved State may in such circumstances resort only to peaceful sanctions.
(iii) The United Nations Charter only forbids the use or threat of force against States, not against peoples or other non-State actors. The Friendly Relations Declaration and the Aggression Declaration include prohibitions on the use of force against peoples, in certain instances.
(iv) The two Declarations also proscribe acquisition of a territory by the use of force. If a State does use force to annex territory, all third-party States are enjoined from recognizing of such territorial expansion.

(v) The two Declarations proscribe the use of force to repel an indirect armed aggression.

4. *Non-intervention in internal and external affairs*

Closely related to sovereignty, the principle of non-intervention is often described as a fundamental principle of international law. Its history extends back to the classical system of international law, and is contained in Article 2(4) of the United Nations Charter, as well as Principles 1 and 2 of the Friendly Relations Declaration. In addition to the Charter's general prohibition on the threat or use of force, the Declaration also forbids any interference by a state against the "political, economic, social and cultural elements" of another state.

The principle purports to be non-derogable and to have universal application. In the Nicaragua Case, the Court declared that the principle consists of three elements:

(i) A State is prohibited to encroach upon the internal affairs of another State by pressuring the governmental bodies of such other States or by interfering in the relations between the citizens and government of such other States.
(ii) A State is prohibited to instigate, organize or officially support activities prejudicial to foreign countries in its territory (for example, supporting the training of rebels).
(iii) States must refrain from assisting insurgents in a civil war breaks in a foreign country.

Source: Nicaragua Case, 1986 I.C.J. 14, at pp. 392–394.

5. *Jus Cogens: Peremptory Norms*

The concept of *"jus cogens"* means that certain rule or principles in international law are so fundamental that they bind all states and do not allow any exceptions. Such rules or principles, called *jus cogens* norms, are also frequently referred to as "peremptory norms" of international law. Although, the concept of *jus cogens* was a subject of controversy for some decades, its inclusion in the VCLT is a clear evidence that it has now been accepted by virtually all states. Article 53 of the VCLT provides the definition of *jus cogens* and the legal implications of such norms:

"A treaty is void if, at the time of its conclusion, it conflicts with a peremptory norm of general international law. For the purposes of the present Convention, a peremptory norm of general international law is a norm accepted and recognized by the international community of States as a whole as a norm from which no derogation is permitted and which can be modified only by a subsequent norm of general international law having the same character."

Article 53 defines a peremptory norm, but gives no examples. No authoritative list of *jus cogens* norms has been adopted by the United Nations or any of its legal organs. However, the International Law Commission [YILC, pp. 247–249 (1966), vol. 2] gave the following examples of *jus cogens:*

(a) a treaty contemplating an unlawful use of force contrary to the principles of the United Nations Charter;
(b) a treaty contemplating the performance of any other act criminal under international law; and
(c) a treaty contemplating or conniving at the commission of acts, such as trade in slaves, piracy or genocide, in the suppression of which every state is called upon to co-operate.

The above examples, though not authoritative or exhaustive, have been widely accepted by international jurists and referred to by governments. In the *Barcelona Traction Case*, the ICJ gave examples of obligations *erga omnes*, which by their nature must also form part of *jus cogens:* "such obligations derive, for example, in contemporary international law, from the outlawing acts of aggression, and of genocide, as also from the principles and rules concerning the basic rights of human person, including protection from slavery and racial discrimination." In the Nicaragua Case, the ICJ stated "the non-use of force as well as non-intervention—the latter as a corollary of equality of States and self-determination—are not only cardinal principles of customary international law but could in addition be recognized as peremptory rules of customary international law which impose obligations on all States."

The legal consequences of *jus cogens* are as follows:

(a) A treaty is void if, at the time of its conclusion, it conflicts with a *jus cogens* norm. (VCLT, Article 53)

(b) If a new norm of jus cogens emerges, any existing treaty which is in conflict with that norm becomes void and terminates. (VCLT, Article 64)

(c) Violations of *jus cogens* will in most cases also be violations of obligations *erga omnes*. In such cases third states may legitimately have recourse to some sort of response.

Source: Encyclopaedia of Public International Law, vol. III, 65–68 (1997); OSCAR SCHACTER, INTERNATIONAL LAW IN THEORY AND PRACTICE, 342–345 (1991); MALCOLM SHAW, INTERNATIONAL LAW, 98–100 (3rd ed. 1991).

6. *The peaceful settlement of disputes*

Article 2(3) of the U.N. Charter imposes on Member States the duty to settle their disputes by peaceful means. Like the prohibition on the use of force, this principle emerged in the international community after the Second World War.

The principle, though sweeping in its language, does not require a particular method or forum for settlement of disputes. Furthermore, a State does not breach the principle by failing to peacefully resolve a dispute if it has acted in good faith.

Though it is fundamental to our understanding of international relations, there is no authoritative evidence of the principle having risen to a preemptory norm of international law.

7. *International cooperation*

The general duty of international cooperation is enunciated in Article 56 of the UN Charter, and is intended to achieve the purposes set forth in Article 55. Although imprecise in its formulation, the main thrust of Article 55 is that States cooperate with one another and, if they fail to do so, must justify their behavior. The principle does not extend to cooperation in relations between hostile countries, one-way assistance or economic aid. It does not have the status of a preemptory norm of international law, but imposes both obligations and rights *erga omnes*.

8. *The principle of jurisdiction*

Jurisdiction is the authority of a state to make, apply and enforce rules within a certain geographic area. Jurisdiction to prescribe law usually precedes jurisdiction to adjudicate, which in turn precedes jurisdiction to enforce. Jurisdiction usually appears linked to territory but not necessarily to control over the territory. Lack of State control and jurisdiction may exist in certain situations, such as during civil wars, or with regard to fishing activities in exclusive economic zones.

The principle of jurisdiction is broken into three types.

(i)   Internal jurisdiction manifests in State immunity from the jurisdiction of foreign courts, or as the right of non-industrialized States to change customary rules concerning the standard of compensation in cases of expropriation of foreign-owned property.

(ii) Boundary jurisdiction differs in that it relates to issues arising at the intersection of an international zone. An example is a boundary rule concerning the breadth of the territorial sea. Another is the right of States to prosecute individuals who are within their custody even though the offence in question was committed outside the territory of the prosecuting State.

(iii) External rules involve restrictions States wish to impose on the freedom of other States to act within the other States' own territories. One example of such external rules in international law is certain human rights obligations. Another is anti-trust legislation, invoked on similar grounds to the second rule identified in the *Lotus Case* and the *United States v Aluminum Co. of America*, but was strongly opposed by most states. In the *Lotus Case*, an act that occurred on board a French ship on the high seas had harmful effects on board a Turkish ship. The act was held to fall within the criminal jurisdiction of the Turkish court. The French captain was in Turkish custody and the Court was given the right to institute its own criminal proceedings. The second rule of the case, namely that an illegal act committed in one State's territory but causing harm in another's falls within the jurisdiction of the second state, was formed in an instance of extreme formalism in the Court's jurisdiction. The Permanent Court seemed to have misjudged the consequences of absence of protest as lack of evidence *of opinio juris* concerning the practice of states abstaining from instituting criminal proceedings. The case, decided by the casting vote of the president, was rejected in Articles in the Convention of the Law of the Sea.

Source: Lotus Case and the *United States v Aluminum Co. of America* 148 F.2d 416, 443 (1945). Byers *Custom. Power and the Power of Rules* 1999. Brownlie, *Principles of Public International Law*, p 7–8.

9.   *The principle of State immunity*

The principle of State immunity entitles a State to immunity from the exercise of the jurisdiction of the national courts in another State. The principle is distinct from the issue of "non-justiciability." When an issue is "non-justiciable," the national court has no competence to assert jurisdiction at all. Immunity, on the other hand, occurs where a national court would have jurisdiction over the subject matter, but is bound to refrain because one of the parties is a foreign sovereign or government. As a result, a judgment of a domestic court cannot be enforced against a foreign state.

The principle of immunity balances the principle of state equality against the principle of exclusive jurisdiction of a state within its own territory. An undue weight in the principle of territorial jurisdiction may render international law ineffective, as enforcement would not likely be available in the defendant-State. This was the holding of Queens Bench in the *Schooner Exchange.*

Its relevance may be explained in the degree to which such enforcement may be regarded as an unfriendly act. Another interpretation of the principle of state immunity is that it is based on international comity.

Source: The Schooner Exchange v McFaddon, 7 Cranch 116 (U.S. Sup. Ct. 1812)

10. *The principle of diplomatic protection*

Every State has the right of "diplomatic protection" of its nationals. The principle is an exception to the principle of exclusive territorial jurisdiction. As a consequence, when a national is injured, the State itself is injured. When a national suffers an injury at the hands of another State, his State of nationality may take up the claim. In the *Mavrommatis Palestine Concessions Case*, the PCIJ stated, "[I]t is an elementary principle of international law that a State is entitled to protect its subjects, when injured by acts contrary to international law committed by another State, from whom they have been unable to obtain satisfaction through ordinary channels." The Court further stated, "By taking up the case of one of its subjects and by resorting to diplomatic action or international judicial proceedings on his behalf, a State is in reality asserting its own right—its right to ensure, in the person of its subjects, respect for the rules of international law."

The principle has certain limitations. A State may only exercise diplomatic protection in respect of foreigners if it is an obligation *erga omnes*. Therefore, international law determines whether a State is entitled to exercise protection. In the absence of sufficient link for diplomatic protection, a court may deny standing to the State. For example in the *Barcelona Traction Case*, the ICJ denied standing to Belgium to assert a claim on behalf of a company which was incorporated and had its head office in Canada, even though a majority (88%) of the shareholders were Belgian nationals. The Court stated that it is a normal rule that the right of diplomatic protection belongs exclusively to the State in which a corporation is incorporated.

The above limitation may not be operative in cases where a treaty permits a State to disregard the issue of nationality and authorizes any party to bring a case. The principle also does not apply where there is a breach of an erga *omnes* obligation.

Source: Brownlie, Ian, *Principles of Public International Law*, 5th ed. Pp. 482–496; *Mavrommatis Palestine Concessions* (Jurisdiction) 1924 P.C.I.J. Ser.A No.2; and *Barcelona Traction Power and Light Co. Case* (Second Phase), 1970 I.C.J. at 605.

11. The principle of personality

The principle of personality usually refers to the capacity of an individual or entity to hold rights and be subject to obligations. In international law, personality of statehood is traditionally seen as the requirement or entitlement to the equal participation of states in the formation of the norms of international law. Thus, a state may object to the formation of a customary norm on the basis of unequal participation of states.

The application of the principle varies from situation to situation. The principle of personality qualifies the equal participation of States when other States in unison influence international norms, for instance as done by developing States on the issue of self-determination. Another qualification, in the context of recognition of States, may occur when States readily recognize the legitimacy of a revolutionary government during a civil war.

Source: Byers, *Custom. Power and the Power of Rules* 1999.

12. The principle of reciprocity (equality before the law)

The law of any society must in principle apply to all its members. In international relations, this concept operates bilaterally only, and the concept of reciprocity is fundamental to bilateralism. It involves the idea that bilateral relationships between at least formally equal parties are not unidirectional, but necessarily involve at least some element of *quid pro* quo. In the context of customary international law, any State claiming a right under international law has to accord all other States the same right. In ensuring that international law accords the same rights to all States, the principle of reciprocity is three-pronged:

A. The principle ensures that States only claim rights it is prepared to see generalized. Thus, the principle of reciprocity qualifies the application of power in the process of customary international law, providing a tool for weaker states to influence the formation of customary law and a tool to purport attempt to develop or change a customary rule.
B. States opposed to a unilateral initiative may respond in negative by engaging in practice supporting the status quo or an alternative rule of law.

States may also refuse to accept a norm by persistently objecting to the unilateral act. But the principle of reciprocity requires that it continue to deal with other States on the basis of the old rule it retains.

13. A State should not allow its territory to be used contrary to the interest of other States

This principle is a corollary of the principle of jurisdiction, and was enunciated in the *Corfu Channel Case*. In this case, mines lying within the territorial water of Albania water had caused damage to a British ship. The ICJ, in holding Albania liable, stated that a State has a duty under international law to prevent any activity that causes damage to another State. A State should not allow its territory to be used contrary to the interest of other States. This principle is very useful in the context of trans-boundary environmental injury. But it can be applicable in other cases as well.

To apply this principle on a different set of facts, consider a case where one State has welcomed a terrorist into its territory. One might argue that a State cannot make its territory a "safe haven" for terrorists who carry out terrorist activities in other States, based upon this principle.

Source: Corfu Channel (U.K. v. Alb.) (Merits) 1949 I.C.J. 4, at 18.

14. Abuse of rights (good faith)

The principle of good faith empowers States with a margin of error in fulfilling their other duties. Some scholars argue that the principle of good faith is superfluous in international law, because it is encompassed by the principle of peaceful co-existence. Nevertheless it is embedded in Article 2(2) of the UN Charter, Article 26 of the VCLT, in the Friendly Relations Declaration, and Article 300 of the UNCLOS. It is fundamental to international relations, because States must have a certain freedom of action in carrying out their obligations, and because the international community lacks courts with compulsory jurisdiction.

The principle states that a State should not exercise its rights in a way so as to cause damage to the rights of other States. Thus, it prescribes how to carry out the performance of a given duty. It is frequently invoked, but has not served as a basis for the decision of the case at issue but as an argument *ad abundantiam* (otherwise expressed) or as an *obiter dictum*.

The principle was discussed in the case concerning *Certain German Interests in Polish Upper Silesia*. Germany had a right to dispose of state property in the territory of Upper Silesia until the transfer of sovereignty established in the peace treaty took place. However, the PCIJ held that a misuse of this right would constitute a breach of Germany's obligation. In the *Nuclear Tests Case* (N.Z. v. Fr.) (1974), the principle served the function of broadening the reach of other legal norms. The principle can also be applicable in respect of liability for lawful acts. Under this principle, compensation might also be sought for the consequence of State actions that are not otherwise unlawful.

Source: Certain German Interests in Polish Upper Silesia (1926), PCIJ, Ser.A, No.7, p. 30; *Free Zones* (1930) PCIJ, Ser.A, no. 24, p. 12; and Brownlie, Ian, *Principles of Public International Law*, at p. 446–448 (5th ed. 1998)

15. Principle of binding obligation of unilateral statement

As a corollary of the principle of reciprocity, a unilateral pronouncement of a State can result in binding international obligations. In the *Nuclear Test Cases*, the ICJ confirmed that unilateral statements could become legally binding. Australia and New Zealand brought a claim against France in respect of the latter's atmospheric nuclear tests conducted in the South Pacific. Before a hearing on the merits could proceed, the French President and Foreign Minister made a series of statements making it clear that France would cease atmospheric testing and the Court considered briefly whether these statements could have created a binding obligation. In the opinion of the Court, "[I]t is well recognized that declarations made by way of unilateral acts concerning legal or factual situations, may have the effect of creating a binding obligations."

If it is the intention of the State when making a unilateral declaration that it should become binding, this is enough to confer upon that State the declaration of a binding legal obligation. Moreover, the majority judgment makes it clear that a *quid pro quo* (reciprocity) is not required, nor is the acceptance, reply or reaction of any other State. It is satisfactory that the declaration is given publicly, either orally or in written form, with intent to be bound.

Source: Nuclear Test Cases (N.Z. v. Fra.) 1974 I.C.J. at 253.

16. Considerations of humanity

Respect for human rights is a fundamental principle of international law. The classical reference is the passage from the judgment of the ICJ in the *Corfu Channel Case* (U.K. v. Alb.) (1949). (the "Corfu Channel Case") In *Corfu Channel*, the Court based its decision in part upon on certain "general and well-recognized principles," including "elementary consideration of humanity, even more exacting in peace than in war."

The exact scope of the principle of consideration of humanity is not yet conclusive. The principle does not impose on States a duty to abide by specific regulations on human rights. Instead, it requires states to refrain from gross violations. In recent years, the provisions of the Article 1(3) of the UN Charter concerning the protection of human rights and fundamental freedoms, and references to "principles" of the Charter, have been used as a more specific basis, for example, in matters of racial discrimination and self-determination.

Some authors subscribe this principle to the category of *jus cogens*.

Source: Corfu Channel (U.K. v. Alb.) (Merits) 1949 I.C.J. 4, at 18. Namibia Case (1971) 57, at 453. *South-West Africa Cases (Eth. v. S.Afr.; Liber. v. S.Afr.)* (2nd phase Judgment) (1966), 1966 I.C.J. 1 at 34 (the "South-West Africa Cases"). Cassese, *International Law in a Divided World*, 1988.

17. The Principle of comity

The principle of comity is also a corollary of the principle of jurisdiction. It requires that, if no evidence of an obligation can be produced, the actions of a State must as a minimum pay due regard to the duty and convenience, and rights of all persons who are under the protection of its laws.

The principle of comity must be used with caution, as it has some limitations. For example, comity was invoked by the United States to justify the extraterritorial effect of its anti-trust laws. Both its anti-trust laws and the invocation of the principle of comity met the massive objection of other States.

Source: Jurisdiction in International Law, ed. W. Michael Reisman 1999. Brownlie, *Principles of Public International Law,* p 29.

18. The principle of legitimate expectations

States are usually held to have consented to the customary rules to which they have acquiesced through shared understanding or legally justifiable expectations. Examples are provided in the principle of unilateral declaration, in the principle of estoppel and the doctrine of *stare decisis.* Economic interests may also serve as a legitimate expectation of States. This principle is evident in the extent of acquiescence in face of claims to the continental shelf and fishing zones. In the *Fisheries Case,* the ICJ justified the special application of the normal rules to the Norwegian coastline, stressing the "certain economic interest peculiar to a region, the reality and importance of which are clearly evidenced by long usage. The principle may also find application in other situations where different interests of states require an element of appreciation, such as those concerning the invalidity of treaties and excuses for delictual conduct.

Source: Fisheries Case, ICJ Rep (1951), 142 and Brownlie, *Public International Law,* p 29.

19. The principle of the supremacy of international law

A State cannot invoke the provisions of its internal law to avoid its international obligations, or as justification for its failure to perform an international obligation. For example, take again the case where State A allowed the adoption of children from State B in violation of its treaty obligation. When State B asks for the return of the children, State A may attempt to argue that, under its federal constitutional system, its federal government has no jurisdiction over adoption matters, as adoption falls within constituent state jurisdiction under its constitution. But under the principle of supremacy of international law, this is a difficult argument. As the PCIJ stated in the *Case Concerning the Polish Nationals in Danzig,* "a State cannot adduce as against another State its own constitution with a view to evading obligations incumbent upon it under international law or treaties in force."

Source: Art. 27 of the VCLT and *Polish Nationals in Danzig* 1931 P.C.I.J., ser.A/B, no.44, p.24.

20. *The principle of pacta sunt servanda*

One rather circular corollary of the principle of legitimate expectations is the rule of *pacta sunt servanda*. The *pacta sunt servanda* rule states that treaties are binding on the parties thereto, and must be performed in good faith. The rule has been the cornerstone of international law from its earliest origin.

The principle is applicable in all-multilateral, regional, bilateral treaties and agreements. Under this principle, a State must act not only in literal accordance with the words of a treaty, but must also act consistent with the spirit of the treaty as dictated by the principle of good faith. The ICJ in its *Advisory Opinion on Reservations to the Genocide Convention* stated that "none of the contracting parties is entitled to frustrate or impair, by means of unilateral decisions or particular agreements the purpose and *raison d'être* of the convention."

Source: Art. 26 of the VCLT; and *Advisory Opinion on Reservations to the Genocide Convention* 1951 I.C.J. p. 21.

21. *The principle of humanitarian intervention*

The very controversial doctrine of humanitarian intervention states that a State may use force in the territory of another State in order to protect the human rights of individuals in this State. It is not necessary for the State invoking humanitarian intervention to claim a link with the individuals in danger. The principle is an alleged general right to intervene with force for humanitarian purposes without the consent of territorial sovereign, as where a government is systematically murdering whole sections of its own population.

Certain preconditions have been set forth for the lawful exercise of this "'right'": for example, the intervention must be authorized by a competent international organization, and the use of armed force is legitimate only in cases of extreme deprivation of fundamental human rights, such as in the case of genocide. However, neither the existence of the right itself, not the conditions for its exercise, is supported by clear state practice.

For example, recently a claim of "humanitarian intervention" appears to have been made by the United States and the United Kingdom as justification for their maintenance of "no-fly" zones in southern and northern Iraq. NATO also attempted to use this doctrine to justify its intervention in Kosovo.

Source: State practice, such as India's intervention in former East Pakistan (Bangladesh) and NATO's intervention in Kosovo.

22. Principles Relating to Defenses to State Responsibility

Although a State is responsible for violation of its international obligation, certain circumstances preclude wrongfulness. They are as follows:

- Act done on the consent of the State (Art.29 of the ILC Articles on State Responsibility (ASR))
- *Force majeure* and fortuitous events (Art.31 of the ASR)
- Distress (Art. 32 of the ASR)
- Necessity (Art.33 of the ASR)
- Self defense (Art. 51 of United Nations Charter)
- Counter-measure/Reprisals (*Naulila Case* (1928) 2 RIAA 1012)

An example of the application of Article 31 of the ILC Articles on State Responsibility can be provided by the *Gill Case,* 5 RIAA 159 (1931). In this case, a British national residing in Mexico had his house destroyed as a result of sudden and unforeseen action by opponents of the Mexican government. The Commission held that the failure to prevent the act was due not to negligence, but to genuine inability to take action in the face of a sudden situation.

Source: Gill 1931, 5 R.I.A.A., at 159; and Articles on State Responsibility.

2. Procedural principles of international law

In addition to the "substantive" fundamental principles, several other principles are frequently invoked in international law. As opposed to the substantive principles, these principles cannot readily claim universal application. Their importance as the basis for a legal argument is supported in each case by the degree of their acceptance. Some are derived from national legal systems, pursuant to Article 38(1)(c) of the ICJ Statute. Others are developed within the context of the international legal system as customary norms or treaty negotiations.

In order to apply one of these general principles, you must first clearly enunciate the principle and identify it as a binding international norm. Principles may be found in passing in decisions and in the writings of jurists, but frequently they do not appear in a context that calls attention to their significance as binding sources of law. To aid you in your search for general principles, some examples on how to recognize a binding principle from a subsidiary source are provided below. Once familiar with the concept of identifying principles, look to describe other principles than the ones mentioned here in your research.

1.   The Principle of obligations erga omnes

An obligations is said to be an "obligation *erga omnes*" when it is an obligation owed to all, rather than just to a particular treaty-partner. The breach of an *erga omnes* obligation is a breach of an obligation owed to each and every state and any group of states. Accordingly any State may object to the breach of such an obligation, by diplomatic protest or, where appropriate, by judicial or arbitration proceedings.

This principle addresses the question of *locus standi* (the right of appearance or standing in a court). Normally when a State appears before an international tribunal, it must first show that it has sufficient legal interest in that case, for example, it may show that the State's own citizens are injured. Ordinarily, a State may not bring a suit on behalf of, for example, non-citizens who have no connection to the State. But the principle of *erga omnes* allows another State to bring a case in situations where the underlying obligation that has been breached has risen to the level of an obligation *erga omnes*. When the principle was first raised, in *the South-West Africa Cases*, the ICJ apparently rejected the notion of obligations *erga omnes*. But further developments, most notably the Court's judgment in the *Case Concerning the Barcelona Traction, Light and Power Company, Limited* (Belg. v. Sp.) (1970) ("Barcelona Traction"), it seems that the Court has changed the position and accepted the existence of obligations *erga omnes*.

It should be noted here that the list of obligations which invoke the principle of *erga omnes* is very short. The doctrine is usually invoked for violations of *jus cogens* norms, but it has also been mentioned in connection with grave and systemic violations of human rights and in cases of environmental protection.

Source: Barcelona Traction (Second Phase), 1970 I.C.J., at 605.

2.   The principle of estoppel

Estoppel is a technical rule of the English law of evidence, and is called "preclusion" in civil law systems. It is a general principle of law recognized by all States. The principle states that a party that has acquiesced in a particular situation or has taken a particular position with respect thereto cannot later act inconsistently with that acquiescence or position. Underlying the formulations of the doctrine of estoppel in international law is that a State ought to be consistent in its attitude to a given factual or legal situation. However, the scope and precise application of this doctrine is not fully developed. To constitute a valid estoppel the following conditions must be present:

(1) The meaning of statement or representation must be clear and unambiguous.
(2) The statement or representation must be voluntary, unconditional and authorized.
(3) There must be reliance in good faith upon the representation of one party, either to the detriment of the party so relying on the statement, or to the advantage of the party making the statement.

The principle has been referred to in disputes respecting the nationality of claims in, for example, the *Canevaro Case*, 11 RIAA 397 (1912) (Harris p.598). The ICJ and its predecessor court, the PCIJ, have pronounced upon the principle of estoppel on several occasions. In both the *Legal Status of Eastern Greenland Case* and the *Fisheries Jurisdiction Case*, the issue of estoppel was raised and the Court did not reject such principle (nor did the court base its decision on the doctrine). In the *Nottebohm Case*, Judge Read invoked estoppel in the common-law sense of estoppel by representation. In the *Temple of Preah Vihear Case*, the ICJ held that by its conduct, Thailand had recognized the very frontier line argued for by Cambodia. International jurists cite this case as an authority for the doctrine of estoppel. In addition in the *North Sea Continental Shelf Cases* and the *Barcelona Traction Case*, the ICJ recognized the doctrine of estoppel.

Sources: George S. Bowett & Sir Alexander K. Turner, *The Law Relating to Estoppel by Representation* (1966); 16 Halsbury's Laws of England 839–947 (Lord Hailsham of St. Marylebone ed., 4th ed. 1992); *Canevaro* (1912) 11 R.I.A.A. 397; *Legal Status of Eastern Greenland* 1933 P.C.I.J. (Ser. A/B) No. 53, at 22]; *Fisheries Jurisdiction* (U.K. v. Ice) (Merits) I.C.J. 1974, at 116; *Nottebohm* (Liec. v. Guat.) 1955 I.C.J., 4]; *Temple of Preah Vihear* (Camb. v. Thai.) 1962 I.C.J., at 6; *North Sea Continental Shelf;* (F.R.G. v. Den. & Neth.) 1969 I.C.J. 3, at pp. 25–26; and *Barcelona Traction Power and Light Co. Case* (Second Phase), 1970 I.C.J.

Estoppel in relation to acquiescence. Acquiescence comes into play when a person remains silent or inactive in a case where, if he did not agree, he would be expected reasonably to voice an objection. Most legal systems are more willing to impose negative duties than positive ones, and an absence of protest other effective action to safeguard established rights is not to be regarded, *prima facie*, as a condition of the continuing validity of these rights. On the other hand, there are situations in which one party's failure to act will prejudice his rights against others who have been misled by that party's inaction or silence. For example, in English law, a duty to object may be postulated where one party, possessing an interest in property, knows that another party, unaware of that interest, purports to obtain an incompatible interest in the same property. When this duty is breached, the silence of a party operates like estoppel, in that he is precluded by his apparent acquiescence from setting up his own interest in the property to defeat the interest acquired by the unknowing purchaser.

Acquiescence produces an estoppel in circumstances where good faith would require that the State concerned take active steps of some kind in order to preserve its right of freedom of action.

Sources: Fundamental Principles of International Law, in Hague Recueils, 87 (1955) pp. 195, p. 256; Christopher Brown, *A Comparative and Critical Assessment of Estoppel in International Law*, University of Miami law Review, 1996, 369–412); and Bowett, *Estoppel before International Tribunals and its Relation to Acquiescence*, British Yearbook of International Law, 1957, vol. 33, 176–202.

3.   *The principle of actori incumbit probandi*

The principle of *actori incumbit onus probandi* (the burden of proof rests on the party who advances a proposition) is a general principle of law and the basic rule of the burden of proof. According to this rule, the party whom makes allegations regarding a disputed fact or issue bears the burden of proving such fact or issue. For example, if the Applicant claims that the Respondent is assisting terrorists in the Applicant's territory, the burden of proof rests upon the Applicant. Similarly a State arguing a certain rule bears the burden of proving that such rule is binding, either as treaty-law or customary international law.

Source: Linda J. Motamed et. al v Iran, Award No. 414-770-2, 3 March 1989, Para.6, reprinted in Iran-US CTR, 28 at 29.

4.   *The principle of circumstantial evidence*

The principle of circumstantial evidence allows the Court to decide a case on the basis of circumstantial evidence. The principle was relied upon in the *Corfu Channel Case*. In this case, the issue was whether the government of Albania had knowledge of anti-ship mines in its territorial water. The Court relied upon circumstantial evidence and stated the following points:

- The fact that certain illegal activities occur in the territory of a State does not necessarily mean that the government of that State has the knowledge of occurrence of such activities. However, a state on whose territory an act contrary to international law has occurred may be called upon to give an explanation, and a reply that the State is ignorant of the circumstances of the act is not sufficient.
- When certain illegal activities that injure other States occur exclusively within the territory of a particular State, it is difficult for other States to furnish direct proof of facts of such activities and the involvement of the government. In such cases, the court will take a more liberal course to inferences of fact and circumstantial evidence. Liability on the basis of circumstantial evidence can only be accepted if there is reasonable certainty and there is one single conclusion as to the use of the evidence.

These are very important points with respect to the question of proof and evidence. In almost every case there is an issue of evidence, and the *Corfu Channel Case* is determining the relative evidentiary burdens of the parties.

Source: Corfu Channel (U.K. v. Alb.) (Merits) 1949 I.C.J. 4, at 18.

5.   The principle of exhaustion of local remedies

It is a well-established rule of customary international law that before international proceedings are instituted based upon an occurrence within a State's jurisdiction, the various remedies provided by the State should first be exhausted. For example, according to Article 22 of Part 1 of the International Law Commission's Articles on State Responsibility, "A State is responsible for injury to foreign nationals only if the aliens (*i.e.* foreign nationals) concerned have exhausted the effective local remedies available to them." However, it is clear that the rule requiring exhaustion of local remedies applies only to cases founded on diplomatic protection and injury to foreign national. If there is a direct State-to-State responsibility, as in case of a breach of treaty involving a State's rights, the matter is immediately and without further action cognizable before the ICJ.

Source: Ambatielos (Grec. V. U.K.) 1956, 83 R.I.A.A.

6. *The doctrine of 'clean hands'*

This principle states that a State that is guilty of illegal conduct itself may be deprived of the necessary *locus standi in judicio*, or standing, to complain of corresponding illegalities on the part of other States. Clean hands is especially relevant if the corresponding illegalities were the consequence of, a response to, or provoked by the illegal conduct of the complaining State.

Justice Schwebel described this principle in his dissenting opinion in the Nicaragua Case. Schwebel observes that Nicaragua is engaged in the same activities as it alleges the U.S. is committing. Therefore, the doctrine of "unclean hands" requires the Court to reject its standing to bring claims against the U.S. Schwebel states that the illegal activities of which the U.S. is accused were embarked upon in order to counter Nicaragua's own actions in El Salvador.

Source: Military and Paramilitary Activities in and against Nicaragua (Nicar. V. U.S.) (Merits), 1986 I.C.J. 14, at pp. 392–394.

VI. How to Apply Policy Arguments and Considerations of Justice

A. *Policy arguments*

Policy justifications often play a crucial role in creating a convincing argument. Policy justifications strengthen legal conclusions reached through more formal means. You might base your argument solely on the narrowly-read rules of international law. But the judges would be more convinced if that rule of law is also supported by policy considerations. Your opponent might challenge your position, supported by equally strong and equally applicable principles of international law. In such cases, policy considerations play a crucial role in the bench's decision as to which rule should be upheld. Additionally, policy considerations may assist in developing new norms or extending an existing norm in a new situation. The ICJ has in a number of cases relied upon policy consideration. These arguments are not extra-legal arguments, because the arguments are found within the law.

To provide the Court with a completely developed legal argument, consider the policy arguments relevant to the issues. To fulfill this task, operate with three different categories of policy arguments: the policy interests of the international legal system; the policy interests of a State; and the identifiable purposes and goals for a specific norm.

The next point to consider is that these categories may only serve their purpose when tested against their desired outcome. The mere reference to "the vital interest of a state" or "the goals of the international community" provides no guidance to the Court. In consequence, open your policy arguments by enunciating the preferable outcome that will result if the Court adopts your position.

1. Policy interests and the basic goals of the international system

Policy arguments that serve to ensure agreed-upon goals of the international community may be relied upon in any argument. They may also be identified as "fundamental principles of international law," as described above, but are not restricted to the principles enumerated in the UN Charter. Other policy lines that have emerged after 1945 may be used; for instance, the right to development.

2. The policy interests of a state

In international law moot court, an argument based on policy interests of the State maximizes your use of the facts. Not every policy decision of a State may serve as a useful policy argument when solving an international dispute. Relevant policy interests are confined to the vital interests of a State, or alternatively, to the *ordre public* of that State.

(i) *The vital interests of States.* The "vital interest of States" is frequently invoked in negotiations and before international tribunals. In one sense the argument of "vital interest" is a necessary corollary of the fundamental principles of international law, most notably, sovereignty, nonintervention and self-determination. Such arguments are confined and tempered by other fundamental principles of international law, such as the consideration of humanity and peaceful settlement of disputes. One viable method of balancing such principles against the vital interest of States is to set a reasonable standard for discretion for States in complying with their rights and obligations (or "good faith").

For instance, assume that a State produces large quantities of a certain mineral that constitutes most of its gross domestic product (GDP). But the refinement of the minerals creates heavy trans-border pollution. This fact may be the basis of a policy argument that the general obligation to limit trans-border pollution must be tempered by the vital economic interests of the State.

The vital interest of a state is a legal argument to be considered by the Court. The Court has in some cases denied the relevance of such arguments, for instance in the *Iceland Fisheries Case* and in the Nicaragua Case.

(ii) *Ordre public.* Another avenue available to invoke the policy lines of a state is to link the policy to the principle of *ordre public*—the fundamental cultural and social values of a state. Reference to the principle of *ordre public* is included as an exemption in most human right treaties and is a basic principle of international law.

Four steps should be taken to make an effective argument for the vital interest or the *ordre public* of a State:

- First, the policy interest in question must be based on an undisputed fact as stipulated in the Compromis.
- Second, the policy interest must be tested against the fundamental principles of international law and other legal obligations.
- Third, the policy interest must meet the test of "reasonable expectations" of the other party.
- Finally, the State's policy interest must be a better solution than other available recourses to secure the main claim.

3. Identifiable purposes and goals for a specific norm

The end result should ensure an application of a particular rule consistent with the purpose of the norm. This is a familiar component in any national legal system, and may be part of international law without any specific consent from the parties.

When building your argument, show how the purpose of the international rule supports your position. On the basis of the facts, explain how your rule fulfills the desired outcome. To further strengthen your argument, bring up points that show how the proposed result will promote the development of international law beyond the specifics of this case.

The *Corfu Channel Case* provides an example of an argument based on policy. A British ship was damaged in the territorial water of Albania, the British government engaged in a unilateral act of intervention by sending its agents to collect evidence of the accident. When the British government tried to justify violation of Albania's territorial integrity, the ICJ denied the right of British government's unilateral act of intervention. The Court stated two policy reasons for this determination. First, acceptance of such unilateral action under international law will often lead to abuse. Second, if such right is accepted, it will be used only by powerful States against weak States. This shows that the Court decided the above issue mainly on the basis of two policy factors.

B. Considerations of justice

Non-substantial legal arguments, or considerations of justice (as mentioned in Section III.D of Ch. 3 and in this Chapter under III.C) may also be part of your legal arguments. Judges may be uncomfortable with an argument based strictly on international rules, unless it is clear where the equities lie. An argument on the existing law applied to the facts may not be enough to convince the judges. The judges want to believe the decision they make is a just one. Therefore, demonstrate to the judges how considerations of justice support your position.

There is some controversy as to the status of considerations of justice under international law. But most accept that ICJ can consider arguments of justice under Art. 38(1)(c) of the ICJ Statute, because justice is part and parcel of every civilized legal system. "Justice" and "equity" in this sense must not be confused with the power of the ICJ to decide a case *ex aequo et bono*, as mentioned in Art.38(2) of the Statute. The power of decision under *ex aequo et bono* can only be invoked by special agreement between the parties, and involves elements of compromise and conciliation. By contrast, considerations of justice are applied as a part of the normal judicial function. Furthermore, under *ex aequo et bono*, the ICJ can disregard the formal sources of international law, but in case of non-substantive legal arguments, the ICJ does not disregard the formal sources, but only makes use of notions of justice and equity to more sensibly and fairly apply them.

VII. How Strict Is the Court's Application of the Sources?

Research will inevitably leave remnants of doubt. A given custom may not have crystallized into a binding rule of international law; treaty obligations may be too imprecise to enjoin a State with rights and obligations in a specific case; or no convincing arguments on policy or justice may be found. Some aspects of the case are just left to the Court, to choose between competing norms.

For the judge, this poses both limitations and possibilities. The institutional position and the general role of the Court limit judicial discretion. On the other hand, the prescribed role of the Court is to develop international law. You should take these limitations and possibilities into account, in arguing for or against a progressive approach to finding law. This consideration is the last element of building a comprehensive legal argument. Determine the application of the following three arguments for judicial activism or judicial restraint on the part of the Court. There are three aspects the Court certainly will consider.

A. Timing

The question of timing raises the issue of whether judicial intervention, taken at this time, will more likely impede or assist international problem solving and conflicts resolution. For instance, in the *Nuclear Tests Cases*, the Court evidently concluded that, at the particular stage then reached in the on-going diplomatic negotiations over nuclear disarmament, no useful purpose would be served by an Court ruling on the substantive legality of nuclear armaments or test explosions. It avoided substantive legal issues by the procedural device of estoppel, holding the French government legally bound by its own previous unilateral declarations of its intention to cease such nuclear tests for the future.

B. Fact finding

The underlying issues of fact do indeed condition or determine questions of ultimate legality, especially where general legal concepts or legal standards are involved. For instance, the fact-finding issue was one of the grounds advanced by the United States in justifying its withdrawal from the proceedings before the ICJ in the Nicaragua Case.

C. Separation of powers

A third possible limit to the judicial activism of the Court is the question of whether other international organs could better determine the issue, or whether a treaty or other instrument specifically reserves the power to adjudicate to another body. In the *Aegean Sea Continental Shelf Case*, the ICJ dispensed with old-fashioned separation-of-powers arguments that would legally inhibit the Court form acting when the Security Council is also acting. Greece unsuccessfully argued that the Court's proceeding should be stopped because of simultaneous action in the Security Council. The Court responded that negotiation and judicial settlement are enumerated together in Article 33 of the UN Charter as means for the peaceful settlement of disputes. In consequence, the fact that negotiations were being actively pursued during the proceeding was not, legally, an obstacle to the exercise by the Court of its official powers. It was in this same spirit that the ICJ, in preliminary determinations in the Nicaragua Case, rejected the U.S. argument that the dispute in question was non-justiciable as belonging to the competence of the Security Council. The jurisprudence of the Court also provides various other examples of cases in which negotiations and recourse to judicial settlement have been pursued without preference by an equal progress.

VIII. Recommended Readings for Research

1. *Encyclopedias on international law*

PARRY AND GRANT (EDS.), ENCYCLOPEDIC DICTIONARY OF INTERNATIONAL LAW (1986).

> This encyclopedia is very useful as it provides simple meanings of each term and further references. It also provides the summary of important documents and international cases.

> The original twelve volumes of this work were published between 1981 and 1990. Each volume covers a broad area of international law and has a title reflecting this area (e.g., "settlement of disputes," "use of force," and "human rights"). It provides detailed commentary on numerous international law topics, cross-references to related topics, and bibliographic references to documentation. Scholarly and authoritative articles on various topics in this area of international law are arranged alphabetically by topic in each volume. The encyclopedia does not have a topical index, but it is possible to know if specific topics are included in the encyclopedia by scanning the title list of articles that is provided in volume 12.

2. *General textbooks on international law*

I.A. SHEARER, STARKE'S INTERNATIONAL LAW (11th ed., 1994).
MARTIN DIXON, TEXTBOOK ON INTERNATIONAL LAW (4th ed. 2000).
THOMAS BUERGENTHAL & SEAN MURPHY, PUBLIC INTERNATIONAL LAW IN A NUTSHELL (3rd ed. 2002).

3. Comprehensive books for advanced research

D.J. HARRIS, CASES AND MATERIALS IN PUBLIC INTERNATIONAL LAW (4th ed. 1991).
IAN BROWNLIE, PRINCIPLES OF PUBLIC INTERNATIONAL LAW (5th ed. 1998).
JENNINGS AND WATTS (EDS.), OPPENHEIM'S INTERNATIONAL LAW, Part 1 and 2 (9th ed. 1992).

> This is an excellent book for research. It provides a select bibliography at the beginning of each topic and its reference to footnotes is very extensive.

LOUIS HENKIN, INTERNATIONAL LAW: POLITICS AND VALUES (1995).
M.N. SHAW, INTERNATIONAL LAW (4th ed. 1997).
OSCAR SCHACHTER, INTERNATIONAL LAW IN THEORY AND PRACTICE (1991).
ROSALYN HIGGINS, PROBLEMS AND PROCESS (1994).

4. Specific books

As an example, on the areas of human rights, some specific books are very useful:

C.G. WEERAMANTRY, HUMAN RIGHTS AND SCIENTIFIC AND TECHNOLOGICAL DEVELOPMENT: STUDIES ON THE AFFIRMATIVE USE OF SCIENCE AND TECHNOLOGY FOR THE FURTHERANCE OF HUMAN RIGHTS (1993)
J.A. ANDREWS & HINES, KEY GUIDE TO INFORMATION SOURCES ON THE INTERNATIONAL PROTECTION OF HUMAN RIGHTS (1987)

> The Andrew & Hines book is a very important sourcebook on the area of human rights. It contains a large number of references to human rights materials published mostly in English.

> If perspectives from authors from different continents are available, use these texts. However, in international law moot court, as opposed in preparation for an academic thesis, it is not expected that you will cite from other than English textbooks.

5. Documentary books for finding treaties

THEODOR MERON, HUMAN RIGHTS IN INTERNATIONAL LAW: LEGAL AND POLICY ISSUES (1985).

BURNS H. WESTON AND OTHERS (EDS.), BASIC DOCUMENTS IN INTERNA-
TIONAL LAW AND WORLD ORDER (2nd ed. 1990).

This is a general documentary book. It has a table of contents
of treaties according to subject matter.

IAN BROWNLIE, BASIC DOCUMENTS IN INTERNATIONAL LAW (4th ed. 1995)

There are also specific documentary books on particular subject matters.

Human Rights:

IAN BROWNLIE (ED.), BASIC DOCUMENTS ON HUMAN RIGHTS (2nd ed.
1992).

Environment:

HARALD HOHMANN (ED.), BASIC DOCUMENTS OF INTERNATIONAL ENVI-
RONMENTAL LAW (Vols. 1–3, 1992).
BIRNIE AND BOYLE, BASIC DOCUMENTS: INTERNATIONAL LAW AND THE
ENVIRONMENT (1995).

International Economic Law:

PHILIP KUNIG AND ET. AL. (EDS.), INTERNATIONAL ECONOMIC LAW: BASIC
DOCUMENTS (1989).

6. Sources for recent developments in treaty law

International Legal Materials (ILM)

This publication provides information and the texts of recent
treaties.

See also "Current Developments in International Law" in American
Journal of International Law and International and Comparative Law
Quarterly. Both provide information about contemporary treaties and
conventions in international law.

League of Nations Treaty series

This work preceded the United Nations Treaty Series and includes
treaties during the period 1920–1945. Many volumes include

indexes. Cumulative indexes are provided approximately every twelve months.

United Nations Treaty series

This collection continues the League of Nations Treaty series. Since it includes most treaties deposited with the UN secretary-general, it is the most comprehensive collection of modern treaties available. Each volume includes indexes. Cumulative indexes are provided for every fifty volumes. The Untied Nations has set up a treaty database on the Internet, available online at *http:// untreaty.un.org/*

7. General books on interpretation of treaties

ARNOLD D.M. MCNAIR, THE LAW OF TREATIES (1961, reprint1998).
I.M. SINCLAIR, THE VIENNA CONVENTION ON THE LAW OF TREATIES (1973).

8. Books on the UN Charter

BRUNO SIMMA (ED.), THE CHARTER OF THE UNITED NATIONS: A COMMENTARY (1994).

This book provides an interpretation of each a8rticle of the Charter, a select bibliography on each article, and useful footnotes.

9. Case books for international law cases

Encyclopedia of Public International Law, Vol. 2 on Decisions of International Courts and Tribunals and International Arbitration.

This encyclopedia summarizes the most important international law cases. It is very useful to get basic information about cases. It provides further reference on the discussion of that case. For example, it provides reference to articles that critically examine the case.

D.J. HARRIS, CASES AND MATERIALS IN PUBLIC INTERNATIONAL LAW (4th ed. 1991).

Harris provides the relevant portions of the important judgments. Cases can be found in the table of cases.

Louis Henkin and et. al. (eds.), International Law: Cases and Materials (2nd ed. 1987).

> Henkin also provides the important portion of the judgments. Cases can be found from the table of cases and the principal cases are in bold type. Note that the last edition is from 1987.

10. *General compilations of cases*

International Law Reports (ILR. Edited by E. Lauterpacht (Earlier titles include: Annual Digest of Public International Law Cases, 1919/1922–1931 and Annual Digest and Report of Public International Law Cases, 1933/34–1949)

> This last work was originally a digest of cases. Since1939 it has also included English-language texts of judgments and advisory opinions of international tribunals, as well as selected cases related to international law from national courts and arbitration awards. Each volume provides a table of cases, table of names, a digest of subjects and keyword indexes. Separate cumulative indexes appear at various intervals. It contains very comprehensive collections of international-law cases.

11. *Courts with general jurisdiction*

> *Permanent Court of International Justice*

Judgments, Orders, and Advisory Opinions, 1930–1940. Series A/B.

> This work continued earlier Series A and B. It is the official chronological publication of full text opinions and orders in French and English on facing pages.

> *International Court of Justice*

Pleadings, Oral Arguments, Documents. The Hague, International Court of Justice, 1947– .

> Bound volumes are separately published for each case. They include written pleadings, transcripts of oral pleadings, correspondence, and other documents in either French or English.

Separate French and English indexes are provided for each case, at the Public Law Institute.

Reports of Judgments, Advisory Opinions and Orders the Hague, International Court of Justice, 1947–.

This annual series contains the official texts of opinions and orders, in English and French on facing pages. Each volume includes a table of contents, list of documents cited, and French and English indexes.

Recent cases from this court are available on the Internet at the ICJ's website, www.icj-cij.org.

Court of Justice of the European Union

Reports of Cases before the Court. Luxembourg, Court of Justice of the European Communities, 1954–.

This work is the official chronological publication of opinions. Annual volumes include a subject index as well as an index of European Union treaty articles. This series is also known as European Court Reports.

12. Human rights courts

European Human Rights Reports. European Law Center, 1979–.

This quarterly publication publishes the decisions of the European Commission on human Rights as well as Judgments from the European Court of Human rights. It includes case, chronological, and subject indexes.

Publication of the European Court of Human Rights, Series A. Judgments and Decisions. Strasbourg, 1974 to present.

Cases are published as separate fascicles with French and English full text of opinions on facing pages.

Publications of the European Court of Human Rights. Series B. Pleadings. Oral arguments and Documents. Strasbourg, 1975–.

This work includes oral and written pleadings and documents arranged chronologically with French and English text on facing pages. Includes separate French and English subject indexes in each volume.

Inter-American Court of Human Rights

Series A: Judgments and Opinions. San Jose, Costa Rica, 1982–.

This work includes Spanish and English full texts of judgments and advisory opinion. Each case is published as separate fascicles.

Series B: Pleadings, Oral Arguments and Documents, San Jose, Costa Rica, 1983–.

This work includes Spanish and English texts of oral and written pleadings and documents, publishes as separate fascicles.

13. Decisions of international arbitration tribunals

Reports of International Arbitral Awards. United Nations. 1948–.

This chronological publication contains the full text of awards from various tribunals in French or English. It includes table of contents in each volume and separate subject indexes in French and English.

Iran-U.S. Claims Tribunal Reports. Grotius Publications, 1981–.

This work includes full text of decisions, awards, and orders. Each volume contains a subject index and numerical, alphabetical, and categorical tables of cases.

Decisions from the International Center for Settlement of Investment Disputes can be found online at http://www.worldbank.org/icsid/cases/cases.htm

14. Decisions from national courts related to international law

British International Law Cases (1964–1970)

This collection of British decisions on international law includes a cumulative index.

American International Law Cases (1971–)

This work contains federal and state decisions concerning international law.

For recent national cases relating to international law—please refer to the appropriate chapter in:
American Journal of International and Comparative Law Quarterly (British)
Other international law yearbooks provide their national cases having significance on International Law.

15. On general principles

BIN CHENG, GENERAL PRINCIPLES OF LAW AS APPLIED BY INTERNATIONAL COURTS AND TRIBUNALS (1953).
Gerald Fitzmaurice, *The General Principles of International Law, 92 Collected Courses, Academy of International Law, the Hague,* (1957 .II) p. 119.

16. On the International Court of Justice

ARTHUR EYFFINGER, THE INTERNATIONAL COURT OF JUSTICE, 1946–1995 (1996).
HOWARD N. MEYER, THE WORLD COURT IN ACTON: JUDGING AMONG THE NATIONS (2002).
SHABTAI ROSENNE, THE WORLD COURT: WHAT IT IS AND HOW IT WORKS (5th ed. 1995).
SHABTAI ROSENNE, THE LAW AND PRACTICE OF THE INTERNATIONAL COURT (3rd ed. 1997).

17. On the International Law Commission

Francis Vallet & Clemens Lerche, *International Law Commission,* in ENCYCLOPEDIA OF PUBLIC INTERNATIONAL LAW 1208–16 (Rudolf Bernhardt ed., vol. II, 2nd ed.. 1992).

A list of reports issued by the ILC, and of conventions based on ILC work. These reports are summarized in the work of the International Law Commission 165-501 U.N. Sales no.E.95.V.6 (1996).

18. *Some of the most important journals and yearbooks that may be consulted*

When possible, use authors from different countries, different legal systems, and different regions of the world. The caveats with respect to language above are valid for journals and yearbooks as well.

Multinational journals:

African Journal of International and Comparative Law
The African Journal of International Law
Australian International Law Journal
East African Journal of Peace and Human Rights
The European Journal of International Law
The Indian Journal of International Law
International and Comparative Law Quarterly
Leiden Journal of International Law
Netherlands International Law Review
Nordic Journal of International Law
The Philippine International Law Journal
Scandinavian Studies in Law
Singapore Journal of International and Comparative Law

United States journals:

American Journal of International Law
Arizona Journal of Intentional Law
Berkley Journal of International Law
Boston College International and Comparative Law Quarterly
Brooklyn Journal of International Law
Case Western Reserve Journal of International Law
Columbia Journal of Transnational Law
Connecticut Journal of International Law
Cornell International Law Journal
Denver Journal of International Law and Policy

Fordham International Law Journal
Georgia Journal of International and Comparative Law
George Washington Journal of International Law
Harvard International Law Journal
Hastings International and Comparative Law review
Houston Journal of International Law
Indiana International and Comparative Law Review
International Lawyer
Michigan Journal of International Law
New York University Journal of International Law and Politics
Stanford Journal of International Law
Texas International Law Journal
Transnational Lawyer
Vanderbilt Journal of Transnational Law
Virginia Journal of International Law
Yale Journal of International Law

Yearbooks:

African Yearbook of International Law
Asian Yearbook of International Law
Australian Yearbook of International Law
Asian Yearbook of International Law
British Yearbook of International Law
Canadian Yearbook of International Law
Chinese Yearbook of International Law
Finnish Yearbook of International Law
German Yearbook of International Law
Hague Yearbook of International Law
Italian Yearbook of International Law
Japanese Annual of International Law
Jewish Yearbook of International Law
Netherlands Yearbook of International Law
Nigerian Annual of International Law
Palestine Yearbook of International Law
Philippine Yearbook of International Law
Polish Yearbook of International Law
South African Yearbook of International Law
Spanish Yearbook of International Law

18. Some useful websites on the Internet

The Internet offers various possibilities for research, both on websites of international organizations and in databases offered by universities and institutes. This collection of web sites is designed to give hints as to where some useful information may be found. Unfortunately, the Internet is a constantly changing medium, and some of the sites mentioned might disappear, might be moved or might be substantially altered. The URLs mentioned were operating as of 23 August 2002.

a. Organizations

A large number of international organizations have established a presence on the Internet. Many of these organizations' websites provide facilities to search material relevant to that organization.

The United Nations

United Nations Organization (UN) http://www.un.org
Official website locator for the United Nations` System of Organizations
    http://www.unsystem.org
International Law Commission (ILC) http://www.un.org/law/ilc
United Nations Treaty Series (UNTS) http://untreaty.un.org/

> This site allows you to search the entire United Nations Treaty Series and the texts of multilateral treaties deposited with the Secretary-General that are not yet published in the UNTS, and to obtain information on the latest participation status of multilateral treaties deposited with the Secretary-General.

Commerce / Trade / Finance

United Nations Commission on International Trade Law (UNCITRAL)
    http://www.uncitral.org
The World Trade Organization (WTO) http://www.wto.org

> The site offers links and sources for research projects; downloading of full-text documents (e.g. Electronic Guide to the WTO and its Agreements) is possible.

International Trade Center, UNCTAD/WTO http://www.intracen.org/itc/

Index to trade information sources on the Internet

Organization for Economic Co-operation and Development (OECD)
    http://www.oecd.org
The World Bank Group http://www.worldbank.org
The International Monetary Fund (IMF) http://www.imf.org
The Multilateral Investment Guarantee Agency (MIGA) http://www.
    miga.org

Lex Mercatoria

http://lexmercatoria.org

> An international/transnational commercial law and e-commerce
> infrastructure monitor by the University of Tromsø. It provides
> links to a great number of treaties, documents and information.
> This database is heavily frequented and might therefore not always
> be accessible. The URLs of mirror pages are:
> http://www.lexmercatoria.net
> http://www.jus.uio.no/lm/toc.html

Additional information may be found at United States International Trade
Commission http://www.usitc.gov

Development

United Nations Department of Technical Cooperation for Development
    http://www.undp.org/tcdc/
United Nations Industrial Development Organization (UNIDO) http://
    www.unido.org
Organization of American States (OAS) http://www.oas.org

Intellectual Property

World Intellectual Property Organization (WIPO)
    http://www.wipo.org

Labor

International Labor Organization (ILO) http://www.ilo.org

Health

World Health Organization (WHO) http://www.who.org

Environment / Sea / Air and Space

United Nations Environment Program (UNEP) http://www.unep.org
The International Maritime Organization (IMO) http://www.imo.org
Center for International Earth Science Information Network (CIESIN)
    http://www.ciesin.org/
Greenpeace http://www.greenpeace.org
Additional information may be found at: http://www.spfo.unibo.it/spolfo/
    SPACELAW.htm

   Research guide to Air and Space Law, treaties, other resources on
   the net.

Cultural Property

United Nations Educational, Scientific and Cultural Organization
    (UNESCO) http://www.unesco.org

Human Rights

UN High Commissioner for Refugees (UNHCR) http://www.unhcr.ch
United Nations Human Rights Committee http://www1.umn.edu/human-
    rts/undocs/undocs.htm

   University of Minnesota, Human Rights Library offers decisions
   and views of the Human Rights Committee rendered pursuant
   to the International Covenant on Civil and Political Rights.

Amnesty International (AI) http://www.amnesty.org
International Committee of the Red Cross (ICRC) http://www.icrc.org

The site of the ICRC offers information concerning implementation of humanitarian rules, documentation and a database.

University of Minnesota, Human Rights Library http://www1.umn.edu/humanrts/

Human rights documents and materials, currently more than 6,000 documents.

Project DIANA Human Rights Archive, Yale Law School http://diana.law.yale.edu

The Orville H Schell, Jr., Center for International Human Rights at Yale Law School offers a search engine and full text documents related to human rights topics.

b. Economic/free trade agreements and organizations

These links to free trade agreements and economic related matters offer access to treaties, statistics and additional information about the different agreements and organization, most of which provide search engines for their servers.

North American Free Trade Agreement (NAFTA)
  http://www.nafta.net/naftagre.htm
  http://www.mexico-trade.com/nafta.html
  http://www.mac.doc.gov/nafta/NAFTA3.HTM

Mercado Común del Sur (MERCOSUR) http://www.netlaw.com/treaties/mercosur.htm

Full text version of the treaty and links concerning the MERCOSUR are at http://www.mercosur.com. Information concerning the MERCOSUR (Spanish)

Free Trade Area of the Americas (FTAA) http://www.ftaa-alca.org

Association of Southeast Asian Nations (ASEAN) http://www.asean.or.id
US-ASEAN Business Council http://www.us-asean.org

Information concerning economic activity in the area of the ASEAN and its member states with links to the ministries of economic affairs.

European Free Trade Association (EFTA) http://www.efta.int/structure/main/index.html
Asia-Pacific Economic Cooperation (APEC) http://www1.apecsec.org.sg
Economic Community of West African States (ECOWAS) http://www.cedeao.org/
The Organization of Petroleum Exporting Countries (OPEC) http://www.opec.org
European Union (EU) http://www.europa.eu.int
G8 Information Centre   http://www.g7.utoronto.ca
Federation of International Trade Associations (FITA) http://www.internationaltrade.org

c.   Dispute settlement and investigative bodies

General

The International Court of Justice (ICJ) http://www.icj-cij.org
World Court Digest, searchable full text versions of judgments of the ICJ http://www.virtual-institute.de/de/wcd/wcd.cfm

Human Rights

European Court of Human Rights (ECHR) http://www.echr.coe.int/
Inter-American Court of Human Rights (IACHR) http://www.corteidh.or.cr/
Asian Human Rights Commission http://www.ahrchk.net/
Human Rights and Equal Opportunity Commission (HREOC) Australia http://www.hreoc.gov.au
European Commissioner for Human Rights (reports) http://www.commissioner.coe.int/

Other Courts

European Court of Justice (ECJ) http://www.curia.eu.int/en/index.htm or http://europa.eu.int/cj/en/index.htm

Judgments of the European Court of Justice
  http://www.curia.eu.int/en/jurisp/index.htm

Other Sources regarding Dispute Resolution

T.M.C. Asser Institute http://www.asser.nl/coop/hague.htm (links to international organizations at The Hague)
International Alternative Dispute Resolution http://www.international-
  adr.com/

d. Journals

Actualité et Droit International http://www.ridi.org/adi/

  A French journal offering fully searchable full text articles analyzing events under the viewpoint of international law.

e. Information from different countries

Often, certain regulations in different countries have to be counterbal-
anced with the situation of the particular state. Under the following URL
such information is provided.

CIA World Factbook 2001 http://www.cia.gov/cia/publications/factbook/

f. Search engines

Most searching on the Internet is done by the use of search engines. It
is, however, not unusual that one of these search engines produces up to
two million hits on one request thus making the result worthless.

  To avoid this, meta-search engines can be used which process the
request through a number of search engines simultaneously. The result
comprises about twenty to sixty hits, which is a manageable quantity.

  An example of these meta-search engines is: http://www.crawler.com

g. Databases

Academic

The N.Y.U. Law Library offers a 'Guide to Foreign and International Legal
  Databases' at http://www.law.nyu.edu/library/foreign_intl/index.html

Commercial

Commercial databanks offer a broad span of pertinent authorities as they include e.g. a great number of decisions, whether reported elsewhere or not in full text. As not all universities are connected to such databanks to which subscription is required, only two are mentioned here.

Lexis/Nexis http://www.lexis-nexis.com
Westlaw http://www.westlaw.com

h. Others

he number of sources on the Internet is far too large to mention all those providing useful information. Only some additional ones that have proved to be useful for conducting research are mentioned below.

American Society of International Law (ASIL) http://www.asil.org

> ASIL provides information through its web site, research library and electronic resource guide.

Max Planck Institute for International Law http://www.virtual-institute.de

> This institute offers links related to public international law and provides the World Court Digest.

Hieros Gamos, The Comprehensive Law and Government Portal http://www.hg.org

The Multilaterals Project http://www.tufts.edu/fletcher/multilaterals.html

> This is an ongoing project at the Fletcher School of Law & Diplomacy of Tufts University in Medford, Massachusetts, to make available the texts of international multilateral conventions and instruments. It includes also historical texts.

i. Link collections

Although a lot of URLs have already been mentioned, there are also superb link collections in the Internet that may prove useful during the research. Out of the large number, only some are mentioned below.

A variety of links related to all areas of international law are to be found on the site of Associate Professor Francis Auburn, University of Western Australia at http://www.law.ecel.uwa.edu.au/intlaw.

Key resources for research in international law on the Internet are provided by Lyonette Louis-Jacques, Foreign and International Law Librarian and Lecturer in Law, University of Chicago Law School, D`Angelo Law Library at http://www.lib.uchicago.edu/~llou/intlaw.html

j.   Other areas of international law

United Nations Crime and Justice Information Network (UNCJIN) http://www.uncjin.org

Center for International Crime Prevention, Office for Drug Control and Crime Prevention

Documents, standards, statistics, countries' laws

UNIDROIT http://www.unidroit.org

Hague Conference on Private International Law http://www.hcch.net/e/index.html

Member states, status of conventions, full text versions of conventions, the Hague Conference is an intergovernmental organization, the purpose of which is to work for the progressive unification of the rules of private international law.

CHAPTER 6

Writing the Memorial

I. Introduction

A. The characteristics of Memorial writing

Although you may continue your research while writing the Memorial, we presuppose that the research is completed at this stage. Writing a Memorial is different from any other legal writing you have previously encountered, such as theoretical presentations or discussing issues arising from a set of facts in an exam situation. The main difference from other legal writing is that Memorial writing requires an argumentative style. The purpose of writing a Memorial is to convince, not merely to describe. As a result, the goal of Memorial writing is to persuade the reader of a position, not to inform of all the possible complexities arising from the issue. Therefore, theoretical writing does not belong in the Memorial, nor does a careful consideration of the position of each party. The role of the advocate is to present the arguments, and only the arguments, that favor the client. Memorial writing is not an academic exercise.

On the other hand, the advocate has certain ethical responsibilities, one of which is to include all authority important to the case, both favorable and unfavorable. The advocate has an obligation to maintain objectivity, as the facts and the law must be given an accurate and complete presentation. In this sense, the writing of a Memorial is very much an academic exercise. To combine the role of academic objectivity and the professional role, the advocate must adopt a persuasive style of writing. Thus, much of the work of writing the Memorial is to organize the material and to formulate strong sentences for a convincing result.

B. The reader

It is important to know and keep your audience in mind. Understand what the reader wants to know and how the reader will react. Keep in mind that the reader wants to have the interesting parts of the case presented. As a result, you need not spend a number of paragraphs explaining the obvious parts of the law. The reader will react to convincing arguments that point to a solution supported by both justice and equity. Human features receive greater attention. Dull syllogisms will not achieve persuasion. Also, the average reader has little patience with poorly-written documents or with Memorials that have poor grammar, spelling and organization.

This is not the place for a general discussion on writing. But the major points of good writing should be kept in mind during the process of Memorial writing:

(i) *Style.* Write short sentences and put each part of the sentence in a logical order. Use the active voice, which is more direct and convincing, wherever possible. Avoid complex language and extended quotations. Short quotations may be used if they are relevant and well expressed.

(ii) *Clarity and precision.* Show that your thoughts are well-organized and follow a logical pattern. Use law and facts accurately, and explain the law of the case.

(iii) *Economy.* Do not spend time on non-controversial points. Focus on contested arguments.

(iv) *Simplicity.* The judges are not experts in all areas of law. Simplicity and adequate explanation is paramount.

(v) *Creativity.* An argument that presents a slightly different twist to the material without distorting the issues will be read with interest. Arguments of equity or policy can be fertile ground for the creative advocate.

(vi) *Professionalism.* Employ a moderate tone in your writing, although your conviction in the case should be clear throughout the pleading. Use proper English, and avoid colloquial terminology.

(vii)*Editing.* In the rewriting stage, a good Memorial becomes a great Memorial. Set aside enough time for editing to achieve the goals above. Cut excess language. Phrases such as "It can be argued" or "It seems that" can be omitted. Check the text for overuse of words such as "We contend" or "We submit."

C. Parts of the Memorial

A Memorial for international law moot court includes seven components. In the finished Memorial the components will be presented in the following order:

Preliminaries (cover page, table of contents and an index of authorities)
Statement of Jurisdiction
Statement of Facts
Questions Presented
Summary of Pleadings
Pleadings
Prayer for Relief

In all likelihood, you will not write the sections of the Memorial in the order in which they appear. For example, most often, you will begin by writing the "Questions Presented" section. In the following all the components of the Memorial will be discussed in the order that they probably will be written, rather than in the order they appear.

II. Questions Presented

The "Questions Presented" section serves three purposes. As with research papers, the Questions Presented identifies the issues and serves to inform the reader about the essence of the case. For these reasons, your questions must be short, precise and be limited in number. They should be understandable on first reading, and be specific to the facts of the case. In addition, you can slant your questions so that they serve as a persuasive device, indicating the favorable answer. For instance, if the issue is on refugee law the Question Presented for the applicant may be formulated as:

> Whether the State of Balboa is properly ensuring the protection of the internationally guaranteed rights of Hillary, her family and the other refugees?

This is an effective formulation because the question suggests that the answer is likely to be no. Furthermore, the question incorporates the given name of the injured. The respondent may formulate the corresponding Question Presented as:

> Whether the State of Balboa has afforded a level of treatment to the refugees, which is consistent with international law?

The language shows that some level of treatment already is afforded, and it suggests that the treatment is consistent with international law. Names of persons are left out.

Note that the claims for relief included in the Compromis may provide a basis for your questions. You should be aware of how your questions relate to the claims for relief. In many cases, there is one question presented per claim for relief. In others, a claim may give rise to two questions. In certain limited circumstances, a question may be germane to more than one claim for relief.

III. The Pleading

The main body of your Memorial is known as the "pleading." In writing the pleading, your main task is to convince the judge to accept your point of view. Your job is to persuade the court that your description of the facts is accurate, and that any inferences you draw from the facts are reasonable. You must convince the judge that the law or rule you have chosen is the most appropriate one, and that your understanding of the law is accurate. Finally, you must convince the judge that your interpretation of the legal landscape and fact pattern is superior to any other interpretation, especially that of an adversary. Pursuing this task, the pleading must include an effective outline, logically structured arguments and argumentative sentences.

A. The outline

The first page every judge turns to in the Memorial is the table of contents. The judge uses the table of contents to become familiar with the structure of your argument. The order in which you present the issues usually follows from the Compromis. If it is not clear from the Compromis, start with the issue that goes to the very heart of the case. When deciding on the order of the arguments within each issue, put your strongest points first.

Decide on a numbering system that is effective. One convention is to give all the issues Roman numerals (I, II, III, etc.), and to denote all supporting arguments within each issue with upper-case letters (A, B, C). Under this system, the further subheadings have Arabic numerals (1, 2, 3) for the particular points under each ground, followed by lowercase letters (a, b, c). If your outline requires lower case letters, you should rethink your outline, as it is probably too complex.

B. The structure of the argument

The next step is to construct the individual arguments. As with the general structure, organization is important. Poor organization can create gaps in the logic and gives your opponents an opening for attack. One of the best ways to organize the argument is to create yet another written outline. Such a "sub-outline" will organize and reorganize your ideas and focus the argument. In addition it will help you spot any gaps or weaknesses in your logic.

1.   The IRAC method for making an outline

The IRAC method (Issue, Rule, Application, Conclusion) is the standard form of policy analysis in preparing a legal argument:

(i) *The Issue.* The issue is the question that this portion of your Memorial serves to answer. In writing your Memorial, the issue is often implied, rather than stated. Ordinarily, the issue will be implied in the section (or subsection) heading, stated as an answer, rather than a conclusion. For this reason, you may want to think of the IRAC method as CRAC (Conclusion, Rule, . . .). Starting with the conclusion is part of a practice of lawyers known as "writing backwards." This benefits the reader because the reader's attention is exclusively focused on the point being made.

(ii) *The Rule.* The rule is the rule-of-law which you ask the Court to apply in this argument. You must both establish the rule in international law and explain the rule. The task is to justify the contention made in the main heading (the issue) with a legal basis. Such basis can come form any source of international law binding upon the parties in the case. Whenever you mention a rule of law, you should include a footnote to the source you are citing.

(iii) *Application.* Next, you should apply the rule you have established to the facts of this specific case. The application connects the law to the facts. In the application, you convince the reader that your analysis is sound and that your conclusions follow logically. As a result, the facts chosen are the ones that are necessary to the conclusion. Refer to the parts of the Compromis you have chosen by citing the Compromis in a footnote, by page and paragraph.

(iv) *The Conclusion.* Unless the argument is very brief (in which case you also need to reconsider the strength of the argument), always conclude. The conclusion, usually only a sentence or two, restates the issue and summarizes the legal discussion.

2. Constructing the logical argument with the IRAC-method

Developing logical arguments is the essence of effective writing. The IRAC method can help convince the reader that your conclusion was developed by means of a tight, well-constructed thought process. It is not easy to create a tight, well-constructed argument at the outset. The complicating factor is that the research process and the writing process are not separate, but inter-linked. The process of creating a pleading involves researching the facts and the law, thinking about the significance of the research, writing up the research, and then going back to do additional research before writing a final draft. Research, thought, and writing are interactive—as you write, you realize that you need more research; as you do more research, what you have written may need to be altered. This makes the task of creating logically structured arguments a bit more challenging.

In order to create a logical structure, think about what you are trying to accomplish when you deal with a problem in law. You will often find that you are trying to establish that a specific set of facts fits within a well-settled rule of law. One way to do this logically and systematically is to use the principles of deductive reasoning to set up the skeleton of your legal analysis. Deductive reasoning is the process that shows a minor premise (a specific situation, event, person or object), fits within the class covered by a major premise (an established rule, principle, or truth), and to prove that the class covered by the major premise must necessarily include the present, specific situation. In Memorial writing, deductive reasoning allows you to prove that your particular case is covered by an established rule. For example:

> *Rule of law (major premise):* International law obligates States to allow minorities to use their own language.
> *Application of facts of the Case (minor premise):* Respondent State has linguistic minorities within its territory and they have been denied the right to speak their language
> *Conclusion:* Respondent State has violated its international obligation.

In fact, the rule, application, conclusion sequence of IRAC forms a simple syllogism: the rule contains the major premise, the application contains the particular facts of the minor premise, and conclusion sums up the information.

3. Adhering to the sources of international law

Making the sources of law (your major premise) fit the specific facts (your minor premise) requires that you flesh out the argument to retain a logical structure. This normally entails explaining the rule in the text. The challenge of writing an international law Memorial is often determining the extent to which the major and the minor premise need to be explained to the reader. Consider the following review of your argument to decide on the extent of explanation to maintain a logical structure:

(i) *The major premise.* International law is to a great extent more indeterminate and raises more issues of when a rule is binding upon the parties than domestic law. In a number of cases where law is developed and certain, you will be able to present your major premise readily as a binding norm. Otherwise, you must extract the rule from a number of sources of international law. Draw the appropriate information from these authorities and present the information showing to what extent the rule is an established rule of international law. The logical demand upon your argument is to show that binding sources of international law in fact support your argument. The only recourse to establish the link between the submission of the ground and the proposition that the rule is binding upon the parties is to show the reader what kind of international law you are applying. If the argument is based on treaty law to which both States are party, it is usually sufficient to remind the reader of the duties imposed upon the parties to a treaty. If the argument requires application of customary law, it is necessary to show this by reference or explicit explanation. If the rule has not yet crystallized into a binding norm of international law, indicate that the evidence only shows the possibility of a customary rule. If the argument is based on general principles of international law, make the necessary link by showing the significance of whether domestic systems, court cases or authors support the existence of the rule. Finally, if the argument is based upon a subsidiary source on international law, show the binding character of the rule, for instance by indicating how a principle pronounced by the ICJ has been repeated by other sources of law.

(ii) *Using analogous facts to link the major and minor premise.* In domestic law in general, and the common law tradition in particular, the technique for expanding your minor premise is by drawing an analogy, either to the facts of other cases or to the policies underlying other decisions. The reasoning is, if two or more situations are the same in some significant respect, they are likely to be the same in other significant respects as well. Therefore, they ought to be classified together. In contrast to common law, international law is a fragmented legal system, and the use of analogies may require some specific support in order to maintain the logical structure in the argument. As a result, show in your argument whether the sources of international law have treated the facts as analogous, or if there are indications that the courts or the States would be likely to treat the cases analogously. If you want to distinguish your case from others, you show that the cases are not analogous, and should not be treated as analogous according to the sources of international law.

(iii) *Using policy arguments to link the major and minor premise.* To argue how the law applies to the facts is often not enough. The advocate needs to persuade the reader that the conclusion provides a just decision. The judges may be uncomfortable with an argument based strictly on authorities, unless it is clear where the equities lie. Put yourself in the position of the judge, and explain why justice will be served if the court accepts your argument. In light of this, another way to link the major and minor premises is to show that the facts of your case are covered by a particular rule because your case furthers the same policy goals as other cases already covered by the rule.

As to the logical structure of the argument, it is important to note that policy arguments may be applied more readily and without any further explanation in national law. Most countries have quite a few common values and collective interests that are agreed upon. In international law, such consensus cannot be assumed. Consequently, to maintain a logical structure, your policy arguments must have a reference to a basic understanding of which considerations may deemed as acceptable by the international community.

(iv) *The conclusion.* When you have established and developed your major and minor premises you are ready to reach a conclusion. This final step should not raise specific problems in international law. As with domestic law, the conclusion follows logically from the premises.

4.   Support the arguments in the text with authorities in the footnotes

In the Memorial it is especially important to support each argument. Therefore, be careful to carry over from the research paper to your Memorial the legal authority which supports each statement of law. The reader should be able to identify whether each sentence or idea is an expression of a binding rule upon the parties, a norm that is not binding but may be applied, or a policy argument or consideration of justice.

Remember that the substantive argument should take place in the text itself, not in the footnotes. To argue in the footnotes is a violation of most moot court competition rules. For example, you can only refer to a case by its proper reference in the footnotes, ("*Barcelona Traction Co. Case*, ICJ Reports, 1970, at page 121"). If your footnote text contains any explanation or description of the case, it will be considered illegal argumentation in the footnotes.

Sample argument employing the IRAC method:

Issue: I. THE ACTS TAKEN BY STATE OF PAGONIA CONSTITUTES UNLAWFUL EXPROPRIATIONS UNDER INTERNATIONAL LAW.

Rule #1: A. The forced divestitures and the cancellation of contracts constitute expropriation.

The term "expropriation" means the deprivation of a right of property by State organs,[1] including courts and administrative agencies,[2] and encompasses cancellation of valid contracts,[3] taking of shares,[4] and so-called forced sales made under the threat of impending expropriation.[5] It is "well established in international law that the decision of a court in fact depriving an owner of the use and benefit of her property may amount to expropriation of such a property that is attributable to the State of that court.[6]

Application: Civil Law No. 51 requires persons holding a majority ownership interest in a regulated entity, a Pagonian commercial entity providing goods and/or services in the cultural sector "to divest themselves of that interest within 90 days," otherwise their interest shall be acquirable by the Pagonian Ministry of Culture. Thus, Bretorian investors were forced to sell their ownership interests, otherwise interests were acquired by Pagonian Ministry through court proceedings.

Conclusion: Thus, the court decisions, in effect depriving the Bretorians of their contractual rights, amount to expropriation.

---

[1]   Brownlie, 531.

[2]   Borchard, 183, 197; *Harvard Draft,* 576; *ILC-Draft Articles on State Responsibility,* Art 6.

[3]   *Norwegian Shipowners' Claims* (Norway v. USA) 1 RIAA 334 (Oct.13, 1922); *Phillips Petroleum Co. Iran v. The Islamic Republic of Iran,* 21 IRAN-USCTR 106 (June 29, 1989); *Southern Pacific Properties (Middle East) Ltd. v. Arab Republic of Egypt,* 106 ILR 628 (May 20, 1992).

[4]   *Amoco International Finance Corp. v Iran,* 15 Iran-USCTR 189 (July 14, 1987); M. Shaw, International Law, 575.

[5]   *Fedorchak Claim,* USA, Foreign Claims Settlement Commission, 40 ILR 96, (April 11, 1962); Christie, *What Constitutes a Taking of Property under International Law?,* 38 BYIL 324 (1962); Higgins, *The Taking of Property in International Law,* 176 RdC 267, 326 (1982 III); Oppenheim's, 917; *Stadt Würzburg v. Intsitut der Englishen Fraulein,* BMV, III US.Ct.Rest.App. 753 (1952).

[6]   *Oil Field of Texas, Inc. And Islamic Rep. of Iran,* 12 Iran-USCTR 318 (Oct.8, 1986); *Decisions de la Commission de Conciliation Franco-Italienne,* Decision No. 196, (France v. Italy) 13 RIAA 438 (Dec.7, 1955); *Barcelona Traction Case,* 105.

Rule #2: B. The expropriations are illegal under international law.

(Here there are three requirements, apply the facts and conclude for each requirement.)

Rule #3: B. Even if the expropriations were lawful, Pagonia is still liable to pay appropriate compensation.

(Explain the rule, Application, Conclusion)

4. Expanding on the IRAC-structure

You may find later on that the complexity of the argument demands an expanded version from the basic structure of IRAC. When the rule is made up of several requirements, build a Rule-Application-Conclusion for each requirement into the main structure. The length and complexity of the discussion will depend upon the importance of the conclusion in the main structure of your Memorial. If the other sections are clear and short then there is no need to restate the conclusion. For instance, if the topic is state responsibility, the following conclusion will suffice:

> Considering that all elements of State responsibility are present and further considering that respondents' claim of defense of necessity is not sustainable, the respondent is thus liable to pay compensation.

Furthermore, an effective argument needs to anticipate counter-arguments. Anticipating, including and addressing likely counter-arguments is important to a high-quality Memorial. List all the ways that one could attack or weaken your argument. After you compile the list, develop responses or rebuttals for each argument on the list. The structure of the argument may end up as Issue-Rule-Application-Rebuttal-Conclusion. Be careful, however, to keep up the argumentative style and to adequately defend against any apparently crippling weakness.

Sample argument expanding on the IRAC—

(for the defense of an alleged copyright violation on the alternative ground that there is a customary rule on the enforcement of intellectual property):

Issue: II. PAGONIA HAS NOT VIOLATED ANY CUSTOMARY INTERNATIONAL LAW CONCERNING THE PROTECTION OF COPYRIGHTS.

Rule # 4: D. The level of protection in Pagonia is consistent with the alleged customary law.

Counter argument: Even assuming that a customary rule exists, adequate protection is offered with the enforcement of the criminal code for intellectual property.

Explaining the rule: The TRIPS-regime reserves the most serious offenses to be punished through criminal sanctions.[7]

Application: Criminal proceedings are available and effective, as they were instituted in at least three of the regions in Pagonia, and considering the underground market only appear in the larger cities.

Policy arguments and legal reasoning: The deterrent effect of criminal sanctions is obvious. Research shows that in fact criminal sanctions are the only form of enforcement that has any such effect.[8] The enforcement is not dependent on the economic situation of the author because he does not have to bear the costs of a civil suit.[9] Criminal sanctions being available, the rightful owner of intellectual property does not have to institute proceedings.[10] Further, considering that the remaining prosecutors can bring actions on copyright infringements, this must be regarded as sufficient standard of protection expected from a least developed country such as Pagonia.[11]

Anticipating counter argument: Assuming *arguendo* that further protection is required, Pagonia does provide the right to remedies. Copyright owners have the right to damages and the right to institute proceedings through a procedure similar to conversion.[12]

---

[7]   Art 61.

[8]   Stewart, supra no.104, at p.83, supra n.90; Julia Cheng, supra no.124 at p.1995

[9]   Carlos A. Villalba, "Penal Sanctions in the International Context: International Criminal Law and Copyright," The Copyright Bulletin, vol. XXVI, No. 3, p.19 at p.26 (1992)

[10]   Compromis p. 7

[11]   Clarifications p.1n.1

[12]   Clarifications p.2 n.15

Application: Pagonia cannot be blamed for the fact that there is no record of anyone being sued civilly after being prosecuted for theft of intellectual property as the decision to bring such cause of action lies solely with the offended copyright owner.

C. Writing argumentative style

The third step of writing the pleading is to formulate argumentative headings and sentences within the paragraph.

1. Writing the headings

The headings are more than titles to specific sections of the pleading. They also appear as the Table of Contents at the beginning of the Memorial. Thus, strongly formulated headings make an initial argument when the judge consults the Table of Contents at different times throughout the reading. As mentioned above, when written in the argumentative style, the IRAC becomes in fact CRAC (Conclusion—Rule-Application-Conclusion). In the process of writing, the advocate usually goes back and rewrites the heading after the argument is structured to achieve an argumentative style. Sub-headings that present the rule also need to be formulated in an argumentative.

The headings should be interesting, informative and easily understood. This is true both for a heading that communicates an issue and a rule. Particularly, the headings expressing the rule should always communicate a point. A "point" is a specific ground for a ruling in favor of the advocate's position. If there is only one ground that supports the issue, it is likely that one point heading for the rule part will suffice. But, often several alternative grounds to defend the position can be argued for instance treaty law, customary international law, and principles of international law. When crafting the headings both for the issues and the rules consider the following:

(i) *The informative heading includes all necessary information.* The headings should inform the judge of the facts, law and logical conclusion. It should help the judge to focus on the argument. If for instance a point heading reads:

> "The State of Balboa has violated international law in altering the flow of the Ozoonio River"

Unfortunately, it does encourage further reading. The judge may also wonder how the advocate got from "altering the flow" to "violating international law." A better formulation, giving a more complete and interesting description of the argument, would be:

> "Balboa is prohibited from altering or diminishing the flow of the Ozoonio River without prior consent of Behestoon."

Now the reader knows the issue to be discussed in the text that follows. The more defined the principle is in the point heading, the more informative it will be.

(ii) *The interesting heading is argumentative.* Consider that one of the purposes of the judge reading the pleadings is to understand the parties' different perspectives as the law applies to the facts. For a merely theoretical approach, other formats than a Memorial would be more suited. Therefore, the judge expects the headings to be argumentative. As a result, the sentences must unequivocally relate the legal position the advocate must take to defend the client. If the heading reads "The protection afforded to the copyright-owners by Pagonia should not be considered sufficient," the judge will be left wondering if the advocate is really convinced of her position. Instead the issue can be stated as follows:

> "The insufficient protection afforded to the copyright-owners by Pagonia is in violation of international law."

(iii) *The easily understood heading is simple and direct.* The heading should be understood in first reading. Focus on the sentence structure by ensuring that the first information reveals what the advocate wants, and thus, the direction of the argument. A simple and direct heading must not be a bare announcement and read: "Copyright infringement." To be easily understood, the heading must be a complete sentence.

2. The sentences within the paragraph

(i) *Use topic sentences.* Start the paragraph with a topic sentence that identifies the main idea discussed in a paragraph. The information will tell the reader where you are going with the sentence. For example:

"Under customary international law, the criminal defendant Malu
Terraq has a fundamental right to a fair trial."

This is a topic sentence. It provides the information that in this paragraph you will be treating customary law with respect to principle of fair
trial and the actions of the State of custody in this regard. Be careful not
to bog down the text with excess words.

(ii) *Use the active voice.* Active sentences are more direct and convincing. Use active voice to show that the other party has violated a principle of law. Describe the actions of the defendant so that they seem real
and direct and it is clear who committed the act. If you write in the passive voice, the focus will be on the act instead of on the person who committed the acts: "International law was violated by Pagonia when the
citizens of Bretoria were denied the full compensation." An active version could be as follows:

The Respondent has violated international law by denying full
compensation to the citizens of the applicant.

To ensure that your sentences are convincing, apply the active voice.
Identify in the sentence the person or institution responsible for a particular action. Use the passive voice only when you are speaking in general terms, when you want to stress the importance of the receiver of the
action, and when you want to downplay or de-emphasize the actor.

(iii) *Make effective word choices.* Full and precise communication of
your thoughts will ultimately depend on the quality of your word choice.
The meanings you attach to the words should be the same meanings that
your readers will attach. Use an English dictionary to check on the meanings of any words about which you are uncertain. Use a thesaurus to find
a word when you are not satisfied with the first word that comes to mind.
You may especially wish to check for situations when specific words or
terms-of-art are used in preference to general words. Short, common
words should be used rather than long, pretentious words. Examine
whether the text in general has more verbs and fewer nouns, and that the
verbs express action and identify the actor, unless the context requires
otherwise.

(iv) *Stating and overstating your case.* Be as affirmative as possible without misleading the court or overstating your authorities. Never use "We think" or "We believe." Pleadings should be written in an impersonal style. Avoid the overuse of "Pagonia pleads," "Pagonia submits," and cut phrases like "we believe," "we feel," etc., as this implies uncertainty in your position.

(v) *Use of quotation.* Although carefully selected quotations can be very effective, do not quote propositions that you can rephrase more precisely or more persuasively in your own language.

IV. Statement of Facts

The facts serve a logical function as well as a tool of persuasion. The Statement of Facts is a presentation of the case that the legal arguments rest upon, and thus a necessary part of any Memorial. The way the facts are presented will influence the judges, as the slanting of the facts is closely inter-linked with the arguments of policy and consideration of justice. An understanding of the facts is an integral part of the outcome of the decision. The importance of a well-written and well-conceived Statement of Facts cannot be over-emphasized. The following present some points to consider when writing the Statement of Facts:

A. The scope of the statement

The content of the Statement of Facts is limited to content of the Compromis. No legal arguments may be contained in the Statement of Facts. Furthermore, you can only draw inferences that lead to one, single conclusion. If the case is about the right to free assembly that was denied in the domestic courts, a necessary inference is that the right to free assembly was officially cut off. This can be part of the Statement of Facts, although it is not expressed in that manner in the Compromis. If possible, you may also add that this fact left the people seeking their rights with no hope of arguing their case through legal and political channels. When a necessary inference is made, cite the record with page and paragraph.

B. Tell the complete story in your own words

A Statement that is merely a recitation of the Compromis will not help the reader to understand the specific of the case needed to apply the rules.

As a result, the Statement of Facts should be a careful selection of the parts of the Compromis required to support the policy arguments and considerations of justice. Rephrase within the scope of the Compromis. In deciding which facts to use and how to present them, accentuate the positive and de-emphasize the negative within the boundaries of accuracy: you can not omit facts that disfavor your case, and you can only draw necessary inferences from the facts. For instance, if the case is about the bombings by some terrorists, who are linked to the country you represent, you cannot omit the fact that there have been bombings.

C. Organization of the facts

The facts can be organized chronologically or topically. The topical approach may be needed if the case is very complex. Whichever strategy is employed, the Statement of Facts should start with presenting the crux of the legal conflict. Begin with the important, favorable and interesting facts. Inform the reader of the nature of the case and the facts to come later. The following beginning on a Statement of Facts for the respondent Pagonia in a case about copyright protection in the Applicant State is *not* a good example on how to introduce the crux of the matter effectively:

> "Pagonia is an agricultural nation with an agrarian and uneducated population and can be classified as a least developed country. Pagonia was established as a young democratic nation after the overthrow of a totalitarian regime in 1975. Pagonia has experienced strong pressure from imported cultural material, and is experiencing a underground market for video and audio-tapes."

Pagonia's status as a young democratic nation and a least developed country is not the essence of the case, and the reader may rightly question the choice of the writer to emphasize on the description of the population as agrarian and uneducated. The case is about copyright protection of the Applicant State as a result of the underground market in Pagonia found in the cities. Consider a more effective approach:

> The Republic of Bretoria has brought a claim before this Court concerning the copyright protection in the Kingdom of Pagonia. In 1996, the World Intellectual Property Organization (WIPO), of which Pagonia is not a member, reported violations of the

rights of foreign copyright owners in Pagonia due to the underground market. Less than a third of the foreign copyright owners with rights allegedly violated, are Bretorian residents.

When the crux of the matter is presented, select to the court the background of the conflict up to the present, if the chronological approach is used. One way to continue would be as follows:

Pagonia is a young democratic nation striving for a private economy after the overthrow of a totalitarian regime in 1975. The easing of the pre-Revolutionary restrictions led to an increase in imports of books, audio- and videocassettes. A result thereof was the trading with unlicensed copies of foreign language audio- and videocassettes in the large cities.

V. Preliminaries

The presentation of preliminary materials is a necessary part of the Memorial. The preliminary materials are:

The cover page
The table of contents
The index of authorities

A. *Cover page*

The cover page consists of your team's number, the name of appellate court to which the Memorial is addressed, the name of the case, year, the name of the parties and an identification of whether the Memorial is for the applicant or the respondent. The precise rules governing the content and format of the cover page are usually enunciated in great detail in the rules of your moot court competition. Follow them to the letter.

B. *Table of contents*

The table of contents consists of all the headings and the sub-headings of your pleadings. It should indicate the page on which each heading and subheading is located. It is also the first opportunity to begin arguing the case. As a result, the layout should be easy to read.

C. Index of Authorities

The index of authorities lists every authority that is cited in footnotes in your Memorial, and the number(s) of each page on which it is cited. The index gives an overview of the sources upon which your argument is based. The index of authorities should be scrupulously accurate. Make the index user friendly by dividing the authorities into headings, usually by type of source (general treaties, specific treaties, UN documents, international cases, domestic cases, NGO-reports, treatises digests and books, journals yearbooks, and "miscellaneous"). Within each heading, list the authorities in alphabetical order. (For style requirements, see Chapter 8).

VI. Statement of Jurisdiction

The Statement of Jurisdiction is a one-paragraph description of the Court's power to decide the case at hand. Jurisdiction follows legally from the agreement in the Compromis and certain articles in the Statute of the International Court of Justice. The presentation is normally a mere formality. Some examples on formulation are presented below..

> The Government of Takkistan and the Government of Suchsdesh have submitted the following dispute by special agreement for settlement to the International Court of Justice pursuant to paragraph 1 of Article 36 of the Statute of the International Court of Justice.
>
> The parties have accepted the compulsory jurisdiction of the International Court of Justice.
>
> The parties submit the present dispute to this Court by special agreement pursuant to Article 36, paragraph 1, of the Statute of the International Court of Justice. In accordance with this article, the two governments have filed a Compromis and agree to accept the decision and orders as final and binding.
>
> The Kingdom of Pagonia and the Republic of Bretoria have recognized as compulsory ipso facto and without special agreement, in relation to any other State accepting the same obligation, the jurisdiction of the International Court of Justice, in conformity with paragraph 1 if Article 36 of the Statute of this Court.

VII. The Prayer for Relief

The Prayer for Relief can, like the statement of jurisdiction, also be viewed as a formality, and can be a reproduction of the claims made in the final paragraphs of the Compromis. The Prayer for Relief, can also be viewed as an additional opportunity to persuade the reader of the points of your case that should not be missed. The Prayer for Relief sums up the whole legal argument. Two somewhat different approaches are provided below; the first is generally considered better form.

> The Government of Pagonia respectfully requests this Honorable Court—
> Declare that the acts taken by Pagonia to protect its cultural identity are consistent with international law,
> Declare that Pagonia is not liable to compensate Bretoria for any injury suffered as a result thereof,
> Declare that the level of protection afforded copyright owners in Pagonia is consistent with international law, and
> Declare further that Pagonia is not liable to compensate Bretoria for any injury occurring as a result of alleged copyright infringements in Pagonia
> Respectfully Submitted
> The Agents
> The Government of Pagonia

or:

> Considering that Takkistan is responsible for the illegal organization of the football league in Sucsdesh;
> Emphasizing that the organization of the football league has caused serious upheaval in the internal affairs of Sucsdesh;
> And further emphasizing that Takkistan has violated its international obligations towards Sucsdesh;
> Sucsdesh respectfully prays that this Honorable Court declare that,
> 1. Sucsdesh has the right to decide its own internal affairs concerning the organization of separate football leagues, and
> 2. Takkistan has violated this right and therefore meddled in Sucsdesh's internal affairs,
> Respectfully Submitted,
> Agents for Sucsdesh

VIII.   Summary of Pleadings

The Summary of Pleadings precedes the actual argument. Because it is
a summary of the body of argument, which itself is subject to review and
revision throughout the writing process, it is most likely that the Summary
the final part of the Memorial that is written. Although the issues may
now be obvious to the writer, the summary of argument is nonetheless
important to the reader. The summary explains the legal nature of the
issues, focuses on the main principles of law and the central sources the
case relies upon. It gives a bird's-eye view of the entire argument in a
few paragraphs; details will be reserved for the pleadings. A mere repetition of the section headings in your Pleadings is arranged is not sufficient for this Summary. Numerous citations are not necessary, but the
most compelling authorities should be included. In this portion of the
Memorial as well, the style of writing is argumentative, for instance:

> This argument is premised on the belief that Ercola has through
> its discriminating public policy deprived the rights of the
> Bretorian copyright owners . . .
>
> The remedy proposed is based on the well-accepted rules of
> State Responsibility . . .

The summary should cover all the central arguments, but not exceed
10% of the pleading section. As an estimate, you will probably find that
a summary that represents 5-7% of the pleading is sufficient.

CHAPTER 7

Preparing the Oral Presentation

I.   The Purpose of the Oral Argument

A.   The prospect

Oral argument is the third part of preparing for international law moot court. Oral argument represents the culmination of your efforts that began with research and continued in writing the Memorial. It is the part that most competitors find the most thrilling.

In international law moot court, you will usually argue the portion of your team's argument on which you have written the Memorial. The issues usually divide neatly into two equally lengthy portions. Usually you have two main issues and several sub-issues. You are to cover both your main issues and the important sub-issues in your oral presentation.

The oral argument is a logical extension of the Memorial. The oral argument is not a duplicate of the arguments in the Memorial, which contains the full and exact exposition of the applicable law applied to the facts of the case. The oral argument compliments the written arguments. It is an opportunity to interest the Court in the arguments laid before the Court, to answer questions and in general to convince the Court of your position.

Oral argument is best thought of as a "conversation." You must persuade the bench of your position, taking into account the bench's questions and your opponent's arguments. Therefore, although the issues presented are the same, each oral presentation is different.

It is essential in preparing for oral presentation to focus on structure and style, in addition to content. The presence of the speaker, in the ability to tailor the argument to the judges' concerns and to formulate responses to questions from the bench, is often the most important feature of a good oral argument.

B. The setting

Oral presentations before any court conform to a formal structure. In international law moot court, the oral argument takes place under strict time limits. The Applicant rises first to introduce the facts of the case, and to explain why the Court should rule in their favor. The Respondent then argues their side of the case, trying to raise counter-arguments to the arguments presented by the Applicant.

II. From the Written to the Oral Argument

In order to transform your written argument into an oral presentation, three steps should be followed. First, evaluate the strengths of the arguments. Second, structure the argument. Third, prepare oral arguments of various lengths, so that you can shorten your argument in response to questions. At the end of this sub-Section, a sample structure of oral arguments is included.

A. Evaluate the arguments

Focusing on the issues to be discussed, decide what you want to argue and in what order. This entails reviewing all of your arguments, the opposing side's likely arguments, and your responses to their arguments. Single out the arguments you believe will stand the greatest chance of being persuasive. Reserve other arguments for use as responses to specific questions. For a systematic evaluation of your arguments, consider the following steps:

1. Sort by issue.

Sort your arguments by issues and sub-issues, list your arguments, the opposing side's arguments, and your responses.

2. Evaluate strengths

Evaluate the persuasiveness of each of your arguments as "strong," "acceptable" or "weak" according to each of three criteria: legal support, factual support and policy attractiveness. You favor those that are strong or acceptable in at least two of the three categories.

3. Considering the opponent's weak points

This is sometimes known as "sabotaging" your opponent's argument. Determine whether any of your opponent's arguments would be difficult or time-consuming to make. Determine what arguments to present (or to omit) in order to require your opponent to address these points. Consider also how your position would be weakened by including or ignoring the point.

4. Considering the opponent's strong points

Some of your opponent's likely arguments will be so important or so obvious that the Court will likely raise them as questions, rather than waiting for your opponent. Identify these arguments. and determine whether it is better to meet these arguments head-on before a question is raised. Alternatively, you may wish to wait until the question arises, and change the focus of the argument. For example, if your opponent has an argument based in human rights, you might re-focus the argument by inviting the Court to solve the issue based on the principle of sovereignty.

5. Considering your own weak points

Often you find that you only have weak support for one of your sub-issues. In moot court, the parties do not have the opportunity to meet and negotiate, and you must prepare to defend all the issues. The bench is aware of this, and it will not be held against you that you are taking a weak position, provided you do not waste the Court's time by overstating the position.

B. *Structuring the speech*

1. Strongest points first

In choosing the order of argument, put your strongest arguments early in the argument. Time is limited, and questioning from the bench may

Sample Worksheet—Evaluation of my argument:

Issue I	Legal Support	Factual Support	Policy attractiveness
Ground #1	S	W	?
Ground #2	P	P	W
Ground #3	W	S	P

Issue I	Legal Support	Factual Support	Policy attractiveness
Ground #1	P	P	S
Ground #2	W	P	S
Ground #3	W	W	P

S = Strong argument
P = Passable argument
W = Weak argument

require you to move to your second issue before you have covered all of your sub-issues. In order to determine which are the strongest arguments, put yourself in the position of the Court. In international law, the Court will need to know to what kinds of cases your proposed rule would extend. As a result the judges are likely to give weight to the policy behind the rule. Given the policy underlying the rule, consider for instance whether the Court would be most likely to choose a treaty-based rule over a rule of customary international law.

2. Emphasize both facts and law

Appropriate attention should be given both to the facts and the law. As in writing the Memorial, the key to an effective oral presentation is the ability to connect the facts with the law. Decide which facts are most important to your case, and include them in your argument.

Some cases may require a closer attention to either the facts or the law. If you are asking the Court to apply new law, emphasis should be given to a discussion of legal arguments. If you ask the Court merely to apply existing law, devote time to apply the facts to the rule, or concentrate on the rules of evidence.

3. Conclusion

The conclusion, or the prayer for relief, should be carefully formulated. It is the final word and the last impression before you leave the stand. In the conclusion restate the orders you wish the Court to make. A brief summarization with an explanation of the relationship between the arguments should suffice.

4. Points on structure particular for the applicant and the respondent

In moot court, the Applicant speaks before the Respondent. However, because the proper role of the Applicant may be more clearly explained after a discussion of the Respondent, we will examine the Respondent's role first.

(i) *The role of the Respondent.* The Respondent has the exciting and challenging task of tailoring its argument to the Applicant's presentation. The Respondent must present its own case-in-chief, but it must do so taking into account the arguments Applicant has made. The Respondent's task is also to undermine each main argument the Applicant has, by negating one or more key sub-arguments. This is one of the most difficult tasks of oral presentation. It is difficult to anticipate the arguments, and the Respondent has very little time during the round to formulate responses to novel arguments. While counsel for the Applicant speaks, take notes of Applicants major and minor arguments, and restructure your speech if necessary. Introduce your position with a correct restatement of the arguments of the opposing side, instead of simply presenting your argument. For example:

> "The opposing party submits that Takkistan's support of the Football Cup constitutes interference in Sucsdesh's internal affairs. Your Excellencies, this is not the case. . ."

or,

> "Sucsdesh alleged that the performance of the speeches depended on the support from Takkistan. Your Excellencies, there is not sufficient evidence to. . ."

or,

> "If I may address another of the elements of the policy arguments put forward by the opposing counsel. . ."

(ii) *The role of the Applicant.* The Applicant must approach the case in a different manner, presenting its own case while anticipating what the Respondent will argue. While the role of the Respondent is to rebut the Applicant's argument step by step, the role of the Applicant is to present the case and, if possible moot the difficult points before the Respondent's presentation.

The Applicant has the first opportunity to present the key facts in the case, and to establish the sources governing the issue as binding upon the parties. If the Court does not question your sources as binding, the Respondent may need to spend time rebutting the application of sources presented by the Applicant before presenting alternative sources.

The Applicant can also incorporate the opponent's written arguments. Insofar as you are aware of the content of the Respondent's argument, refute rules that you view as non-binding, and distinguish rules or cases that do not apply to the case. Alternatively, moot the Respondent by refocusing the issues, as described above.

(iii) *Counter-strategies for the Respondent.* The Respondent should refute important misrepresentations of facts and law the Applicant has made, but should not spend much time on these points. Focus the attention of the Bench on the outcome of the case, not on sweeping discussions of international law. Instead of attacking Applicant's submissions on one ground thoroughly, a better strategy may be to reveal many small doubts about the strength of the Applicant's case. For instance, you might question the policy arguments presented by the opposing counsel, and then focus on introducing alternative sources.

(iv) *Rebuttal.* Rebuttal and surrebuttal are the opportunity for the Applicant and Respondent, respectively, to respond to the arguments of the opposing council. In form, its purpose is to be short. In international law moot court, an effective rebuttal is usually not more than 3 to 5 minutes.

The content of rebuttal and surrebuttal is limited, by rule and by custom. The Applicant's rebuttal must be directly responsive to points the Respondent made in its argument-in-chief. The Respondent's surrebuttal must be directly responsive to points the Applicant made in its rebuttal. If you attempt to raise points your opponent did not raise in its immediately preceding argument, the Bench may stop you or, worse yet, may allow you to proceed but take points from your score.

Another consequence of this rule is that if Applicant waives (decides not to take) rebuttal, Respondent automatically waives surrebuttal. Therefore, Applicant may strategically choose to waive rebuttal, in order to avoid allowing Respondent another opportunity to speak.

Not all misstatements or arguments of the Respondent can be addressed in the short time allowed for Applicant's rebuttal. If the Applicant's work in anticipating counter arguments in the main was well done, there should not be a long list of points to choose from for the rebuttal. Only a few important points you need to re-address should remain.

Some advocates rely on an opportunity to argue for shock value in the rebuttal. This strong hand approach consists solely of identifying wrong use of cases or breaches in the logic of the argument. The approach is dependent on a significantly poor and reckless quality of the opponent's presentation, and may easily backfire if you are perceived by the bench as being aggressive merely for the sake of being aggressive.

The preferred approach is to choose as the topic for the rebuttal the points most necessary for resolution of the case. This approach focuses more on the communication with the judges and entails that you decide ahead of time on issue to bring up in the rebuttal. Identify the issue that is pivotal to your case. It may be the issue that you cannot afford to allow the judges to decide in a strictly legal positivistic manner. Or it may be the issue that can create the greatest imbalance between the parties. If you do decide on a rebuttal topic ahead of time, be mindful that if Respondent does not raise the issue, you cannot raise it on rebuttal. More subtly, watch to see whether the judges are interested in your topic. If the judges do not seem to care about your proposed rebuttal topic during the arguments-in-chief, you may wish to consider changing your topic or waiving rebuttal.

Open the rebuttal and end it correctly. At the outset, address the Court and identify your issue, explaining why and when Respondent put the issue "into play." For example:

"Your Excellencies, Applicant submits one issue for rebuttal. During its argument, counsel for Respondent stated that the framework of sovereignty has changed since 1945. Applicant contests this submission. . ."

Enumerate the reasons why the Court should decide on this issue in your favor. Go through the reasons within the very strict time limit. Use the opportunity to stress complex legal issues in a clear manner, and bring forth your thoughtfully formulated policy considerations in full force. If there is time, end the rebuttal by reiterating the request for relief.

(v) *Particular points on surrebuttal.* During surrebuttal the Respondent needs to be acute as to its scope, as the surrebuttal must be strictly responsive to Applicant's rebuttal. Much like rebuttal, a surrebuttal must also be pointed and focused. Even if the applicant's rebuttal brought up several issues, and the Respondent is permitted to be equally broad, this is not advisable. The respondent also does well then, by determining ahead of time which issue is pivotal to the case.

In addition to being focused, the Respondent also has the task of distinguishing his argument in only a few words. Particularly if the Applicant's rebuttal managed to strike a pose between an appropriate level of forcefulness and well-stated perspectives of how the law should be applied, it may be a good strategy to start with conceding the weight of the Applicant's argument. This changes the pace for a moment, and allows you to build up a crescendo. If you start forceful after a strong rebuttal, the judges may be taken aback, and you will have a much more difficult time distinguishing your arguments. Proceed by showing how the forceful arguments of the Applicant do not completely address the equally strong arguments that support your position. Remember to conclude.

C. *Time management and restructuring during presentation*

Your time is limited and the line of questioning can undermine your carefully planned structure. Depending on the circumstances, you will have about 20 to 30 minutes to present your case. When your time is up, you must thank the Court for its attention and sit down, even if you did not cover all of your issues. As a result, be prepared to shorten your oral presentation without losing your structure. In this regard, consider employing the following techniques:

1. Rate the arguments

Divide each argument under each issue or sub-issue into necessary, important and convincing arguments.

(i) *The necessary arguments.* The necessary arguments are absolutely central to the understanding of your case. They must be presented in one or two sentences. They include the conclusion and the source supporting the rule.

(ii) *Important arguments.* The important arguments are arguments of law, facts or policy that explain the rule, and should be covered, or at least listed if time is short.

(iii) *The arguments of conviction.* The arguments of conviction are those that buttress your position, including alternative grounds for a conclusion or additional sources supporting a sub-issue. You will probably not be able to cover all of these during a hard line of questioning, but they can be an effective way to return to the original structure if they can be incorporated in to the answers. When answering questions, find ways to include your alternative arguments into the questions from the bench.

(iv) *Save time for questions.* Do not stuff your speech with too many arguments. Anticipate questions and revise your outline, taking into account time spent answering questions from a hot bench.
A worksheet to assist you in structuring your argument is included below.

2.   Divide the time between your main issues

If you spend too much time is spent on answering questions before you have started explaining the rules governing the first issue, you have wasted time which might be spent later in your argument. Prepare a short version of the important arguments governing the first issue and only list the arguments of conviction. If you receive no further questions on the first issue, turn to the second issue, and proceed with your necessary and important arguments. During the argument, adjust the level of detail according to the number of questions you receive and the amount of time remaining.

3.   Save time for prayer for relief

You are required to conclude your oral presentation in some fashion. You do not want to miss the opportunity to reaffirm your position to the bench. As a result, without rushing the judges, be sure to save time to properly conclude or sum up your case. If time is very short, even if you have not covered important arguments governing the second issue, immediately turn to a short version of the prayer for relief.

Worksheet—Strategies for time management:

The "short version" is the argument one uses before a "hot bench." The "full version" incorporates all of the elements of the short version, and also includes some convincing arguments to fill time before a "cold bench."

Issue I	Sub-issue	Rating for short version	Rating for full version
Ground #1	1st requirement	N	
	2nd requirement	N	
	2nd req. theory a & b		C
	3rd requirement	I	
	Application of facts	N	
	Policy		C
Ground #2	Treaty wording	N	
	Application of facts	N	
	Policy	I	
	ICJ case supporting treaty interpretation	I	
	Application of facts	I	
	Domestic cases supporting treaty interpretation		C
	Application of facts		C
Ground #3	Evidence of custom in bilateral treaties		C
	Ex. in international affairs		N
	Application of facts		I
	Policy		I
Issue II	Sub-issue	Rating for short version	Rating for full version
Ground #1	Conclusion	Short version	Full version

N = Necessary argument, I = Important argument, C = Convincing argument

D. Sample structure of an oral argument

The following is one model outline for your oral argument. The basic structure is the same as the Memorial: state your conclusion first and then support it with facts and law. The opposite approach is often too complex for the listener to follow.

Variation #1:
— Address the Court and introduce yourself and your client.
— Present the two issues to be discussed.
— State your claim on each issue.
— Perspective. Give the importance of the case.
— If necessary, present the facts from the Compromis which are most pertinent to the issues.

Turn to the first submission (issue):

First ground:
• Introduce the first rule of law governing the first issue.,
• Explain the rule, determine the content of the "right"
• Apply the facts relating to the rule
• Dispel exceptions.
• Conclude

Second ground:
• Explain the rule etc.
• Apply the facts
• Dispel exceptions
• Conclude

Turn to the second submission: (issue):
• Repeat the steps for the first issue.
• Prayer for relief.

Variation #2:
— Address the Court and introduce yourself and your client.
— Perspective. Give the importance of the case.
— Present the two issues to be discussed.
— State the claim on each issue.

Turn to the first submission (issue):

First ground:
* Introduce the first rule of law governing the first issue.,
* Explain the rule,; determine the content of the "right"
* Apply the facts relating to the rule
* Dispel exceptions.
* Conclude

Second ground:
* Explain the rule etc.
* Apply the facts
* Dispel exceptions . . .
* Conclude.

Turn to the second submission: (issue):
— Repeat the process above. Prayer for relief.

III. Techniques for Effective Oral Presentation

Oral advocacy is thought indispensable to the court system to illuminate complicated cases. The purpose of oral argument is to enhance, explain and support your written pleadings. Merely repeating your written arguments aloud does not enhance the Court's understanding of your case. This Section will present some techniques that the judges will look for, including style of the speaker, clarity of presentation, persuasiveness and attitude towards the court. At the end of the Section, some customs on word-usage are included.

A. *Requirements on style*

When preparing and delivering your oral presentation, you must be mindful of certain rules of style. The following is general advice that applies to oral presentations in almost any context:

(i) *Do not merely read from a prepared text.* Reading a previously-written speech defeats the purpose of the oral presentation and is dreadfully boring. Although you might prepare a full oral argument during practice and preparation, you should only bring with you to the podium an annotated outline of your argument, consisting of the major points of your argument and certain sub-arguments, citations and support.

(ii) *Do not merely memorize a prepared argument.* Much like reading, merely reciting a prepared text defeats the purpose of oral argument, and is boring for your listeners. In addition, it is difficult to interact with the judges and to react to your opponents' arguments when you are merely reciting a canned speech. During practice, you should decide on the major points you want to make, and then prepare several different ways of making them.

(iii) *Maintain eye contact with each of the judges.* This is essential. Draw each judge into the "conversation" by slowly moving your eyes from the one end of the bench to the other. When answering a question from a particular judge, you should address your answer primarily to the judge who asked the question, but be sure not to exclude the other judges.

(iv) *Use inflection and proper emphasis.* A monotonous speech can be very difficult to follow. Proper emphasis on words or phrases can show the listener what your priorities are and can show your conviction for your client and case.

(v) *Use pauses.* Speak a little more slowly than in everyday conversation. Use pauses judiciously to stress the points being made and to allow the judges to reflect upon your words.

(vi) *Keep a natural, composed posture.* Try to preserve your natural body language when speaking. Do not make exaggerated motions with your hands, and do not sway or pace back and forth. By the same token, a stiff speaker can be just as distracting as a speaker who sways from side to side. Therefore, remain relaxed and keep your bodily motions natural.

B. Clarity in presentation of the material

A proper oral presentation must also adhere to certain points regarding organization. Bear in mind that this is the first time the judges have heard your argument, and it is harder for them to follow your argument than it is for you to deliver it. In addition, you may be using legal terminology or nuances with which the judges may be unfamiliar. The following points on presentation of the content are essential to any oral argument:

(i) *Outline your argument.* At the beginning of your presentation, give the judges an idea of the overall outline of your argument. Note the claims you will be addressing, and the general bases for each claim. By introducing the judges to the structure of your argument, you prepare them for the substance of your argument. As you turn to each individual argument, it is easier for the judges to follow the details of your arguments. By the time you come to each new argument, the direction of your speech is at this point already familiar to the bench.

(ii) *Structure your sentences in a simple manner.* Simply structured sentences are easier to listen to than complex, compound, or run-on sentences. Bear in mind, however, that the spoken word is more informal than the written word. While run-on sentences may hamper a written text, run-on sentences, used sparingly, can sometimes serve as an effective tool to capture attention in oral speech.

(iii) *Use repetition.* As a courtesy to the bench, repeat your legal conclusion after you have finished a section of your argument. This provides the judges with an opportunity to question you further about the topic, and provides constant reminders about the bases for your arguments. This is especially important when you switch from one issue to the next.

C. *Persuasiveness*

Remember that even an oral presentation with all the features described above has its limitations. An oral presentation may easily be perceived as a monologue if the speaker does not invite interaction from the listeners.

In international law moot court, the goal of the presentation is to convince the bench, and an involved judge is a better listener. Persuasive speaking requires a certain heartfelt commitment and dedication to the case. If you are unsure you can muster the proper commitment, be careful when employing the following techniques, as you do not want to appear an insincere, overzealous advocate:

1.   Take a stand

At the outset of your speech, give the bench an overall theme upon which your arguments rest, basing your argument (and, if possible, that of your co-Agent) within a larger context. The bench should immediately recognize and identify your position. Your emotional perspective should also be evident. Usually, a perspective can be achieved by describing the importance of the case. For example:

> "The question before the Court today is of crucial importance to the world trade. . ."

or

> "Today, the Court, by granting the relief that Takkistan seeks, will give effect to a universal affirmation of the right to self-determination. . ."

2.   Adopt a conversational style

To engage the judges in the argument through questions and answers, the effective advocate employs a comfortable, conversational style of speaking. The advocate can not directly ask questions of the judges. Even rhetorical questions may be perceived as an improper breach of decorum. The manner in which to engage the bench is to adopt a conversational style. Do not "bully" the bench with every possible citation or argument in support of each point; give some support, and allow the bench to ask for additional support or explanation. In worst case, such a "bullying" approach may be perceived as condescending. Instead, engage the bench with a calm and confident presentation showing the clarity of your structure.

3.   Tailor your speech to the judges concerns

Do not belabor the obvious, as it will bore the judges. If a point is uncontested—or if the judges appear to fully understand or accept your point, go on to your next point. Similarly, if a judge wishes to discuss an argument you had planned to address later, do not hesitate to change the order of your argument and address the judge's concern immediately. Such flexibility shows your appreciation of the judge's questions, which is what you want to encourage.

4.   Answer the judges' questions

Nothing is more frustrating for a judge than an unresponsive oralist. You should, in every event, attempt to answer a question directly and immediately. Even when the answer hurts your argument, you should at least have the courtesy to answer the judge first. You can follow your answer with your exceptions and counterarguments, but the first words out of your mouth should be a direct answer—"yes" or "no" when called for.

Even a simple yes or no questions from the bench often prove very difficult to answer. If the judge's question is unclear or poorly phrased, ask the judge for clarification to make sure of the point the judge is making. For example;

> "Is Your Excellency asking whether bilateral treaties can be evidence of customary international law?"

This method contains an added benefit. When the judge clarifies the question, you may find that the clarification gives you a different perspective on the issue, which you may be able to more easily answer. Remember that the overall goal of answering questions from the bench is persuasion through conversation.

5. Do not interrupt the judges

Be certain that the judge has finished the question before you start answering. A "hot" bench can challenge your patience, but you must allow the judges to finish their sentences. On occasion, a judge may include two questions is a single statement, or a judge may "piggyback" a question on another judge's question. In this case, indicate to the bench that you have heard more than one question, and indicate the order in which you will address them. Then answer each question separately.

6. Be a little provocative

When you are faced with a "cold" bench, you may have to provoke the bench into participating. Carefully and mildly overstate your case where the facts are clear. This may challenge the bench to question you about the case. Be aware that this is a dangerous strategy: you must only provoke the judges when you know you can defend your overstatement, or at least retreat with dignity. Be willing to tone down your choice of words if the judges make indications for you to do so.

D. Attitude towards the Court

Your attitude towards the Court should be one of appropriate respect and deference. The helpful, attentive advocate will be at an advantage. As a result, do not treat any words from the bench as obvious or as a waste of time. Respond empathetically to the bench. Even during repeated interruptions or unending hard-line questioning, you should be both receptive and cooperative. An irritated or aggressive response will only annoy the judges.

On the other hand, the judges expect a deferential advocate, not a servile advocate. To avoid a subdued appearance, give definite answers. Be confident in the strength of the argument, and clear on your position. Speak with a positive tone. In short, your attitude towards the bench should be one of respectful equality.

Give your opponent due deference as well. If your opponent miscites a case or misrepresents a point of law, only bring such mistakes to the Court's attention during your argument if they are material to the case. If you do bring such mistakes to the Court's attention, focus on the mistake made, not the person who made it. Do not accuse your opponents of intentionally misrepresenting the law. If the point is minor or an obvious misunderstanding of international law, you have no obligation to correct the statement.

E. Word-usage

A few customs of formal conduct should be observed in the oral argument:

1.   Never use first-person pronouns

The words "I" and "we" should almost never pass your lips when you are presenting an oral argument. First of all, remember that you are representing your client—you are not the client. Therefore, "We submit" is less preferred than "Applicant submits" or "Takkistan submits." The phrase "I think" is almost never appropriate. Rather than, "I think that the rule supports this claim," say, "The rule supports our claim," or, if you are unsure, "The rule would appear to support this claim."

2.   The opening

When beginning the argument the speakers should rise and say;

> "M. President, members of the Court, my name is . . . and I appear here in the Court with my co-agent, . . . , for the applicant state. . ."

or

"May it please the Court, my name is . . . I appear on behalf of the Applicant in this case. Appearing with me is my co-agent. . ."

2. The outline

Note that you "submit" an issue or an argument for the Court. The phrase is "It is submitted," "Takkistan submits" or, less preferred, "We submit." As mentioned above, you should never say, "I submit." You can also "present" or "deliver" a submission.

You "turn" or "move" to your first submission, or from one submission to the next. You can for instance say "I will now move to the second submission under the first basic issue."

You may have a first, second or third ground or points (rules) that your claim is based upon. For each ground you may have requirements that must be met in order to invoke the rule.

3. Opposing counsel

As a matter of professional courtesy, opposing counsel should be referred to by name or as "agent for the defendant," or, in some circumstances, as "our Honorable friends." Do not refer to opposing counsel as "my opponent."

For a strong approach, refer to your opposing counsel's arguments (but not your own) as "contentions," "assertions" or "positions."

4. The arguments

An action can be or not be "in consonance with" or "in accordance with" international law. A principle may or may not "bear upon" an item in the facts.

You may state that the opposing party "has breached international law," that they "can not escape its obligations," or that a violation "gives rise to the duty to make reparation."

You may state that your client has not "violated" the rule of international law, or "has no duty" to act in a certain way. Your opposing party may "dispel to satisfy the burden of proof," or they "have not presented sufficient evidence to support the position."

5. Refer to sources

You may need to refer to a treaty or an organization with a cumbersome name and wish to use an abbreviated form or an acronym. The first time you refer to such an organization or instrument, state the full and proper name, and then say "which I will hereinafter refer to as WTO" or "I will be referring to as the 1970 Friendly Relations Declaration."

Refer the Court to articles in treaties or paragraphs in decisions:

> "If I may refer your Excellencies to article 18 in the Vienna Law of Treaties. . ."

Within the article of a treaty, the article may have sections and sub-sections. For instance, Article 1(2) if the United Nations Charter should be read as, "Article 1, Paragraph 2." For an added effect you may want to introduce two instruments as one:

> "The right of self-determination which we find in the 1960 General Assembly resolution 1514 on the declaration of independence to colonial territories has been basically reproduced in principle 5 of the 1970 General Assembly resolution on Principles with Regard to Friendly Relations."

When introducing a principle you may use the following:

> "Your Excellencies, I am referring to the principle of *uti possidetis,* or "ownership to the possessor," which is a general principle of international law as established by the *Frontier Dispute Case,*"

or

> "By supporting a separatist group, Takkistan is interfering in the internal affairs of Sucsdesh. The principle in non-intervention is a principle of customary international law, as espoused in the Nicaragua Case. In paragraph 206 of that case, the Court specifically states that a state shall not. . ."

For the last example, notice how you introduce case law. When rebutting the application of a principle made by the opposing party, consider:

"Agent for the applicant relied upon circumstantial evidence, and they correctly referred to the *Corfu Channel Case* as an applicable authority. However, in that case, this Court also held that when inferences of facts were drawn upon circumstantial evidence, those inferences must leave no room for reasonable doubt."

When referring to the Compromis use "as is stated in paragraph six in the Compromis," "the Compromis clearly shows," "it is not evident from the Compromis," or "nothing in the Compromis indicates."

6. Answering questions

In answering questions, address the judge as "Your Excellency" or "Your Honor." Again, never start an answer in first person, "I believe" or "my position is." Instead, refer to your argument as "Takkistan's submission," or say, "it is submitted" or, less preferred, "we submit that."

Whenever possible, begin by answering the judge's question "yes" or "no." If the judge presents you with an opposing argument, acknowledge the argument before turning to your argument:

"Yes, Your Excellency, it is true that the principle of self-determination was developed in the colonial context, but even in. . ."

or

"Certainly, it will always be a risk that the principle of self-determination will be exploited, however. . . ,"

7. Conclusion

When stating your prayer for relief, consider the following:

"Filova respectfully requests the Court to declare the terrorist act as illegal and to order compensation for the human lives lost."

You end the speech with "that concludes my submissions" or, "if there are no further questions, that concludes my submissions." You may wish to conclude your argument by reciting the prayer for relief contained in the Compromis. If you choose to do so, make sure not to change key words or recharacterize the pleadings, as this may be seen as an attempt to deceive the Court.

IV. Preparing for Questions by the Court

Much has already been said on the importance of questions and answers, as they permeate high-level oral advocacy. In supplement to the principles presented above, some particular points on effective answers and categories of question follows. Some sample questions are provided at the end of the Chapter.

A. *Effective answers*

Questions from the bench may reveal the judges' perceptions, biases, areas of expertise, and concerns. Some questions are designed to support your view, others are simply points on which the judge has no preconceived opinion. As previously stated, the most important task is to answer the question adequately. To give a prompt answer is not of great importance. Therefore, it is often wise to pause and rethink your answer, to avoid confusing the bench further with a disorganized answer. Evasive or non-responsive answers usually provoke judges to restate the question.

In order not to get stuck on a certain point, you may want to blend your answer with your next point and thereby advance in your argument. Make smooth transitions to the next point and you will maintain continuity in your presentation. If the question is of minor importance and time is running out, you may concede to minor points. This is especially true if by conceding a minor point, you can convince the judges of your reasonableness, and thereby gain their trust on a major point.

B. *Categories of questions*

1.   Questions on rules of law

(i) *Questions on particular points of the rule.* Judges may ask questions on particular legal arguments for a variety of purposes. The judge may be concerned with the logic of the argument, that the statements are precise, and that your analogies are not too broad. Use the knowledge you have acquired through research to address the concerns of the judge.

(ii) *Questions to test your knowledge.* A judge may also ask questions on particular legal arguments to test your knowledge of the case and depth of your understanding. Such questions are sometimes formulated as "slippery slope" arguments, "the worst possible case scenario," or as a list of the possible negative implications the rule may result in. Do not be discouraged and think that the judge is unfavorable to your argument. Instead, admit to the difficulties and turn the questions into an interesting discussion on how to resolve the issues.

(iii) *Questions on the "why's" of the rule.* If the judge asks hypothetical questions, the motivation may be to test the further implications of your argument. The questions can be formulated as "if the Court rules in your favor . . ." or "what are the long-term outcomes if the rule is applied. . ." Your task is to present your strongest policy arguments to open for a discussion of the policies underlying the rule.

2. Questions on authorities cited

(i) *Questions on application of sources.* If the judge asks questions about an authority you have presented, the question concerns more than facts of the case and the content of the rule. The important part is as always, the context of the original rule and on how the source relates to the case at hand.

(ii) *Questions on strength of the argument.* The judge may also be concerned to what extent the source is binding upon the parties in the case, if the source show the development of a rule of international law, whether a valid exception may be made, or why the source is persuasive (a policy question).

3. Questions on the facts

When presented with questions concerning the facts, the judges usually want to know which facts are crucial to the case. It may also be a friendly hint that your argument has wandered too far from the facts of the case.

V. Practice Sessions

In order to know your speech by heart you need to rehearse. Speak in front of a mirror for your ordinary practice sessions. When you start to know your argument, try it out on friends or classmates. You may wish to test the clarity of your argument by asking a friend who is not familiar with the law to listen. Listeners who are not lawyers should be able to understand the essence of your case.

When you are ready, recruit professors, your teammates, or other specialists to serve as a "practice bench." Practice in front of hot and cold benches, switch to the arguments of the opposing side, employ a slightly different style, and sit as a judge yourself. If you have the opportunity, videotape your performance.

VI. Some Frequently Asked Questions for Oral Presentation

It is not possible to anticipate all questions you will be asked in the competition, but some questions on the fundamentals of international law are frequently asked are provided below. Formulate your own answers. An example of a dialogue between an advocate and a panel of judges, complete with answers is also provided.

1. Are the sources mentioned in Article 38 of the Statue of the ICJ exhaustive?
2. Is there any priority or hierarchy of sources of international law?
3. What is customary international law? What are the elements of customary international law? How is it proven?
4. What is *opinio juris*? How is it proven?
5. Where can we find evidence of State Practice?
6. How long has a rule to be practiced before it becomes a customary norm?
7. What is *jus cogens*?
8. What is the doctrine of *Stare decisis*? Is ICJ bound by its earlier decisions?
9. What is the status under international law of resolutions of the United Nations General Assembly?
10. What is 'soft law'?
11. What is *travaux preparatoires*?
12. Who can appear before ICJ?
13. What is the process for an Advisory Opinion of the ICJ?
14. What are the remedies available in international law?
15. How can the ICJ quantify the damages asked for?
16. How can a decision of the ICJ be enforced?
17. What is "justice"?
18. If all things are equal, what criteria should we apply to make the choice?
19. What is the standard of proof? Which party bears the burden of proof?

VII. Sample Dialogue

The dialogue is taken from the Championship Round of a recent year's Phillip C. Jessup International Law Moot Court Competition. To convey a realistic picture of a international law moot court dialogue, this dialogue includes some of the inaccuracies—present for even the most prominent speakers—in the spoken language.)

> *Q: Counsel, are the three General Assembly resolutions [which counsel had previous cited] constitutive of international law, of a lawmaking nature?*

Your excellencies, a General Assembly resolution in itself is not legally binding, however, in the *Nicaragua* case, this court, in paragraph 188, has stated that where it is sufficient state practice and opinio juris, that a General Assembly resolution can become customary international law . . .

And we submit on the strength of 3 resolutions, adopted all without dissent, this constitutes customary international law, in fact this has been further supported most recently in 1996 at the peacemakers summit in Egypt.

In that summit we recognize that not all states were present, in fact, only 31 states were present. However, the states that are most particularly affected by terrorists acts, because they in the past had supported it, or because they had also suffered under terrorist attacks. For example: The USA, Egypt, Qatar, Kuwait, United Arabic Emirates, and all these countries came together to condemn terrorism.

That whatever the motivation, whoever the perpetrators, terrorist acts must be eliminated, this we submit is evidence, is clear evidence of customary international law, of this legal obligation in international law to suppress terrorism.

We ask this court to translate or interpret this obligation and hold that Filova must declare YLSA illegal to carry out this obligation

> *Q: Are you suggesting to this Court, Agent, that if we cannot find the norm in international law that is not already created, this court has the power to create an international law norm?*

Your Excellencies, may I ask which international law norm, is it to suppress terrorism?

> *Q: That is what you are saying . . .*

Yes, Your Excellencies, indeed this court does look to previous precedent, does look to state practice as in Article 38 of the statues of this court.

But this court can create law. It can create law when it is shown that states desire, that states have united to condemn terrorism, and this court must create law to give effect to that condemnation of terrorism . . .

But as my submission has already been Your Excellencies, there is already in existence this customary international duty, an obligation on states to suppress terrorism.

And we ask this court to apply that duty to Filova, and hold that it has indeed breached international law in its refusal to declare YLSA illegal

Q: Are you saying to this Court that we should apply U.S. law?
No, Your Excellencies. This is the ICJ and it will apply international law as it sees fit.

However, domestic law can constitute a general principle of law where courts in many countries in the world follow the same principle.

And under Article 38 of the statutes of this court the court would look to that.

In any case this also shows state practice and is again a source of law which this court will look towards

Q: Are you saying that if this court, deciding this case, cannot find any treaty law, any hard law, then we are prevented to create the norm that would be applicable to this case?
The court is not limited to finding norms of international law based on treaty or hard law, as the court looks to other source of international law primarily state practice.

However, it is submitted that the agents of the applicant have not produced any in this court and that none exist in this particular area

Q: And are you saying that state practice cannot be inferred from the fact that a number of states have gathered to condemn terrorist acts and terrorist groups
The court could infer that there is a rule that states must condemned terrorism, however unless states have actually banned terrorist organizations, there it does not appear to be any practice that states to that effect.

Furthermore, briefly on the question of whether or not Filova has violated the duty, there is no evidence that Filova knew or could have known that YLSA was operating from within its territory. Ercola has not been able to stop its terrorist acts. It does seem to be any reason why Filova should be able to either . . .

And, when this court in the *Corfu Channel Case* was discussing the due diligence obligations of Albania. . . . The court there was concerned with a situation where Albania was responsible for the supervision of the Corfu Channel. Which is a strip of water along the coast of which it had many observation platforms, there is no such observation platforms for watching over terrorist activities,

If I may turn then to my fourth submission, which is that Ercola has violated the Yttics [interrupted by judge]

Q: Just one moment. . . . Agent, where do you find the justification of what you just asserted before the Court? What is the rationale of your argument? Where can this Court find the actual law to give you what you are actually asking from this Court?

Your Excellency, if I may refer your to principle 5 of the 1970 Friendly Relations Declaration, it describes peoples here and as we have defined, peoples must have a distinct territorial link

More pertinently, your excellencies, I will refer you to paragraph 7 of this declaration, which states that nothing in the right of self-determination is to authorize the impairment of territorial integrity

In other words your Excellency, after the peoples have gained independence, after de-colonization has occurred, there is to be no further right to impair territorial integrity

This your excellencies, I am referring to the principle of *uti possidetis* which is a general principle of international law as established by the *Frontier Dispute Case.*

Q: Counsel, doesn't that principle refer to inter-state claims, but is it a principle which does not bear on the question of whether within a state a group may succeed?

Your Excellency, it is *true* that the principle of self-determination was developed in the colonial context, but even in the post-colonial context.

This is after the peoples have attained self-determination. Peoples have attained independence.

The Vienna Declaration of 1993 as well as in the 1994 General Assembly resolution 49151 still hold that the right of self-determination must be limited to peoples with a link to a distinct territory under alien subrogation, colonial domination or foreign occupation.

No further right accrues, Your Excellencies, to a minority group within an independent state.

Q: Counsel, can you really maintain that the right of self-determination is one that derives only from the independence movement from colonialism where the right of self-determination first came to the fore?

Your Excellency, it is true that self-determination did begin from the colonial context, but there are good reasons why the law has held extremely firmly that these colonial boundaries must remain or if they do not remain, we are looking at a situation of international instability of contested borders

For example Your Excellencies, if we were to say that the peoples of West Firland have a right of self-determination, then the Yttics in the rest of Ercola would not be given this right

Q: Are your suggesting counsel, that we should follow a doctrinal approach to international law, as the precedent . . . as the norm to give binding force?

No Your Excellency, the words of the 1970 Friendly Relations Declarations are clear and we must uphold them today because of the rise of post-modern tribalism

Q: If I may ask you, counsel, which of the national liberation movements that we have seen in the recent decades have been elected by the people they purport to represent?

Your Excellency, that is a difficult question to answer because you are right in that, peoples do not often come forward to endorse these groups, unless they are well established, such as the Palestine Liberation Organization

But your Excellencies, on the facts here, the Yttic people have a right of political participation

Q: But the right to vote, does that not include the right to put up candidates for elections?

Indeed, Your Excellency, and the Yttics have this right, they can put up any candidates. Except, I stress again Your Excellencies, except the political party cannot espouse separatist ideology.

Q: It seems that you suggest that the right of self-determination exist only where the people claiming the right have a distinct link to a separate territory. It seems possible to me that, if a people have a distinct territory under its control, it is already enjoying

self-determination. Then, of what or in what does the right of self-determination exist?

Your Excellency, the right of self-determination is a right for these groups of peoples to freely determine their political status.

This means that they can choose to secede to establish an independent nation or to integrate with another nation this is found in paragraph 4 of principle 5 describing the modes of self-determination. There is no restriction on what these peoples can do, this is why a [interrupted by judge]

Q: Am I to understand. . . . As your government has put out a large, a very large number of military, and you have prescription and you have all kinds of ways to bring young people into the military . . .

We have as evidence before this court an annex, and in this annex I see that you are asking the ethnic group among other things that might be divertible. But lets focus on one particular item, how can you explain that this document, done much before if I understand correctly, before the emergency powers you are claiming now, as being possible under international law?

Your Excellency, you are asking me whether it is illegal in international law whether it is illegal to ask for a group to state their ethnicity on a form

Q: And I am also asking you why your government thought it necessary to do so?

Your Excellency. . . . Now, the database is a very complex compilation of military data and we use it for a variety of reasons, as listed in page 3 of the Compromis, we use this data to assign . . . [interrupted by judge]

Q: So you keep speaking of a subversive group as the defendant of the proceeding as a state . . .

How do you make the connection from a subversive group to another state, because you have to attribute the one to the other?

Indeed, Your Excellencies, we are not saying that Filova is responsible for the acts. We are saying that they are responsible in international law, because they have gone beyond political, moral and humanitarian assistance. They have gone beyond that, they have breached the principle of nonintervention, and I have four facts to show how they have gone beyond those limits by supporting this organization

Q: Counsel is it anything in that declaration that obliges a foreign state to declare illegal under its law a foreign terrorist movement assuming arguendo that this movement is such?

Your Excellencies, no. However, there is a general duty, a legal obligation in international law today that states must cooperate to suppress terrorism . . .

And this can be found in the same declaration. It can also be found in the 1985 declaration against terrorism, in the 1983 resolution against human rights and terrorism. All these three resolutions, which were all adopted without dissenting states, express that states must come together to condemn and eliminate terrorism. This is the duty in international law, and we submit that the most effective way, and the simplest way. [interrupted by judge]

Q: Counsel, do you have facts other that the ones accounted a moment ago by your colleague to support the proposition that what you characterize as terrorism is in fact operating from the territory of Filova?

Your Excellencies, our case is not that Filova is responsible for state sponsored terrorism. We are not saying that YLSA has carried out its terrorist attacks, the bombing of the stock exchange and the train station, from Filovan territory. It is not supported by the facts if that was our case.

Our case is wherever those terrorist facts may have occurred, the fact of the matter is that YLSA, or elements of YLSA have gone into Filova, and therefore Filova must declare YLSA illegal.

Q: I understand, your position seems to be that what Filova should to fulfill its duty to stamp out terrorism is something they should do when perpetrators of Ercolan acts arrive in Filova?

Yes, Your Excellencies. If I may move on to my second submission . . .

CHAPTER 8

Citation of Authorities

I. General points
II. Some short forms
III. Basic rules for citations

I. General Points

In Memorial writing, cite an authority or authorities to show support for a legal or factual proposition or argument. Each legal proposition or sentence contained in the text must be supported by authorities.

The foremost function of a citation is to enable the reader to find the authority in the library. Make sure that the citation is accurate and in the form required by the rules of the competition. Moreover, a citation provides the reader with enough information to make an initial decision about the authority's importance or weight. Your credibility as a legal analyst relies, in part, on the correct use of citations. The incorrect use of citations may detract from an otherwise well-written Memorial.

Citations can be placed either in endnotes or footnotes. The use of footnotes is recommended. It is more convenient, as the reader can see the authority cited on the same page as the principal for which it is cited.

One general rule for using footnotes or endnotes is to write the textual part of the document so that it stands on its own. That is, the reader should be able to follow the text without looking at the citations. As a consequence, there must not be any subsequent argumentation in the notes. The notes should only be used to give the correct citation of the authority presented in the text.

There is no general rule as to the number of authorities you must cite in support of your argument. Normally, when you have simply stated a well-settled proposition in the text, one authoritative citation is enough. For example, the principle that when a State violates its international obligation, it must make reparation needs only one citation.[1] The proposition is undisputed and supported by the decision of the P.C.I.J. (the Permanent Court of International Justice, predecessor organ to the ICJ) itself. More authorities are needed where you make proposition that is disputed. For example, if you wish to state that copyright law is part of human rights, you should recognize that this issue is highly contentious and not yet settled. In this instance, you must cite a number of authorities that support this conclusion.

II. Some Short Forms

With respect to footnotes, there are several conventions worth mentioning. You may already have familiarized yourself with some of them through the research.

A. The use of Id

Id. is short for *idem*, which means the same as previously given or mentioned. Therefore, use '*Id*' when citing to the immediately preceding authority. It should not be used when there are intervening footnotes citing other sources. Some examples follow:

1. RAJ BHALA, INTERNATIONAL TRADE LAW: THEORY AND PRACTICE (2d ed. 2001)
2. *Id* (same page)
3. *Id* at 543 (different page)

B. The use of Supra

Supra is Latin for "above." When an authority has been fully cited previously, the *supra* may be used (unless *Id* is appropriate). Remember *supra* may be troublesome in case you change the number of footnote in last minute. If you use *supra*, make sure the footnote number is correct. Example:
22. BHALA, *supra* note 1, at 166.

---

[1]   *Chorzow Factory* (Ger. v. Pol.) (Merits), 1928 P.C.I.J. (ser.A) No.17, at 29.

C. The use of op.cit

In the research papers it is convenient to use "op.cit.," or opposing citations to keep in mind other approaches. Other manners in which opposing citation is signaled is by "But cf." "Cf." Literally means "compare."

D. The use of Hereinafter

For authority that would be cumbersome to cite with the usual *supra* form, or for which the regular shortened form might be confusing to the reader, a shortened from may be established. For many of the long titles of international instruments, there are unofficial, common ways to shorten them. Especially for treaties, General Assembly Resolutions and international cases, it is better to use 'hereinafter' than *supra*.

The common abbreviations may for instance be found in textbooks. After the first citation of authority, place the word 'hereinafter' and the special shortened from in brackets:

Montreal Protocol on Substances That Deplete the Ozone Layer, Sep.16, 1987, art.7, 26 I.L.M.1550 (entered into force Jan.1, 1989) (hereinafter Ozone Layer Convention).

III. Basic Rules for Citations

The form that is used here is taken primarily from the *Uniform System of Citation*, widely known as the "Bluebook," published by the Harvard Law Review Association. You are not required to utilize the Bluebook system, but once you select a particular form of citation, you should follow it consistently throughout the entire Memorial.

Some examples of citation are as follows:

• *United Nations Charter*

Art. 2, para. 4, Charter of the United Nations, June 26, 1945, 24 U.S.T. 2225, 3 Bevans 20 [hereinafter U.N. Charter].
Art. 6, U.N. Charter.

• *International Treaties*

First find the United Nations Treaty Series (hereinafter U.N.T.S.) number:
Montreal Protocol on Substances That Deplete the Ozone Layer,

Sep.16, 1987, art.7, 226 U.N.T.S.161 (entered into force Jan.1, 1989).

If the treaty is not found in U.N.T.S., provide a citation to International Legal Materials (hereinafter I.L.M.):

Montreal Protocol on Substances That Deplete the Ozone Layer, Sep.16, 1987, art.7, 26 I.L.M.1550

(entered into force Jan.1, 1989).

- *General Assembly Resolutions*

Principles of International Co-operation in the Detention, Arrest, Extradition, and Punishment of Persons Guilty of War Crimes and Crimes against Humanity, G.A. Res. 3074, U.N. GAOR, 28th Sess., Supp. No. 30, U.N. Doc. A/3926 (1973).

- *International Law cases: ICJ and PCIJ*

The citation of international cases consists of a case name, the parties' names, volume number and name of publication and date:

Military and Paramilitary Activities (Nicar. v. U.S.), 1986 I.C.J. 4 (June 27) (separate opinion of Judge Ago)

Diversion of water from the Meuse (Neth. v. Belg.), 1937 P.C.I.J. (ser. A/B) No.70, at 7 (June 28)

A detailed explanation follows, as this can be difficult to do correctly if you do not have the proper citation already provided in a legal text:

Case name:

Give the case name as found on the first pages of the report, but omit introductory articles such as "The." Also omit the word "case," unless the case name is a person's name. Do not otherwise abbreviate case names. For instance, write "Nuclear Tests," not "Nuclear Tests Case." Then when writing in the case name, use italics.

Parties' names:

The names of the parties involved should be given in a paren-thetical phrase immediately following the case name. You can abbreviate the names of the parties. The Blue book has provided how countries should be abbreviated (see T. 11 of the Bluebook at p. 311 of the Seventeenth Edition). However, there is no harm in giving the full name of the parties.

Advisory opinion:

In advisory opinions, no parties are listed. Here you cannot abbre-viate the countries as they are part of a case name: *Interoperation of Peace Treaties with Bulgaria, Hungary and Romania*, 1950 I.C.J.65 (Mar. 30).

Volume number and name of publication:

Identify the volume by the date on its spine: 1972 I.C.J.12

The name of the publication of the I.C.J. is: *Report of Judgments, Advisory Opinions and Orders*

Decisions and other documents of the P.C.I.J. were published in six series (A through F). The series must be indicated in any cita-tion to P.C.I.J. documents: 1937 P.C.I.J. (ser. A/B) No. 70

Page or case number:

Cite I.C.J. cases to the page on which they begin. Cite cases of P.C.I.J. by number: 1937 P.C.I.J. (ser. A/B) No. 70.

Use pinpoint cites to refer to specific pages: 1937 P.C.I.J. (ser. A/B) No. 70, at 12

Date:

Provide the exact date, where available: *Nuclear Tests* (N.Z. v. Fr.), 1973 I.C.J. 135 (Interim Protection Order of June 22)

Putting this in to the Memorial, suppose in the text, you have made the following argument:

"The International Court of Justice has confirmed that the principle of non-intervention has achieved the status of customary international law."

The correct citation in the footnote would appear as:

16. *Military and Paramilitary Activities* (Nicar. v. U.S.), 1986 I.C.J. 4, at 47 (June 27) (separate opinion of Judge Ago).

17. *Diversion of water from the Meuse* (Neth. v.Belg.), 1937 P.C.I.J. (ser.A/B) No.70, at 7 (June 28).

Separately published pleadings:

The pleadings before the I.C.J. are published separately in *Pleadings, Oral Arguments, Documents* (abbreviated I.C.J. Pleadings), while those before P.C.I.J. were published in P.C.I.J:

Memorial of the United Kingdom (U.K. v. Alb.), 1949 I.C.J. Pleadings (1 Corfu Channel) 17 (Sep. 30, 1947).

Memorial of Denmark, Legal status of Eastern Greenland (Den. v. Nor.), 1933 P.C.I.J. (ser. C) No.62, at 12 (Oct.31, 1931).

- *Court of Justice of the European Communities*

Pre-1990 cases:

Case 111/79, *Caterpillar Overseas v. Belgium*, 1980 E.C.R.773.

Post-1990 cases:

Case C-213/89, *The Queen v. Secretary of State for Transport ex parte Factortame Ltd.*, 1990 E.C.R. I-2433, [1990] 3 C.M.L.R 1 (1990).

- *European Court of Human Rights*

Ireland v. United Kingdom, 23 Eur. Ct. H.R. (ser. B) at 23 (1976).

•   *European Commission of Human Rights*

The cases can be published in different publications and examples are given accordingly:

Y. v. The Netherlands, App.No.7245/32, 32 Eur. Comm'n H.R. Dec. & Rep. 345, 358 (1982).
Smith v. Belgium, App. No. 3324/76, 8 Eur. H.R. Rep. 445, 478 (1982) (Commission report).
Iversen v. Norway, 1963 Y.B. Eur. Conv. on H.R. 278 (Eur. Comm'n on H.R.).

•   *International Cases in National Courts*

International Law Reports normally publish decisions of various national courts that have relevance in international law. The cases should be cited as follows:

Abdul Ghani v. Subedar Shoedar Khan, 38 I.L.R. 3 (W. Pak. High Ct. 1964).

•   *Domestic Sources*

Constitutions:

U.S. CONST. art.1, § 9, cl. 2.
U.S. CONST. amend, XIV, § 2.
Or, Bangladesh Constitution art. 21.

Statutes:

National Environmental Policy Act of 1969 § 102, 42 U.S.C. § 4332 (1994) (U.S.).
Emergency Power Act, No.3 (1975) (Ir.)
CODE CIVIL art. 1112 (Fr.)

National cases:

If jurisdiction is not clear indicate parenthetically the jurisdiction:

United States v. Montoya de Hernandez, 473 U.S.531 (1985).

R v. Bow Street Metropolitan Stipendiary Magistrate, ex parte Pinochet Ugarte (No 3) [1999] 2 WLR 827 (U.K.).

• *Books*

Always give the author's full name as it appears on the publication. Use "at" if the page number may be confused with another part of the citation; use a comma to set off "at" from preceding numerals:

IAN BROWNLIE, PRINCIPLES OF PUBLIC INTERNATIONAL LAW 445 (5th ed. 1998).

If there are two authors:

RAJ BHALA & KEVIN KENNEDY, WORLD TRADE LAW: THE GATT-WTO SYSTEM, REGIONAL ARRANGEMENTS, AND U.S. LAW 147, 243-45 (1998).

If a work has more than two authors, use the first author's name followed by 'ET AL.'

A. LEO LEVIN ET. AL., DISPUTE RESOLUTION DEVICES IN A DEMO-CRATIC SOCIETY 80 (1985).

• *Articles*

Bernard H. Oxman, *Complementary Agreements and Compulsory Jurisdiction*, 95 AM J. INT'L L. 277, 285 (2001). [Note that T. 14 of the Bluebook at page 317 of the Seventeenth Edition provides a list of aberrations of journals].

• *Articles in a Book or Shorter Works in Collection*:

Maria Del Lujan Flores, *The Scope of Customary International Law on the Question of Liability and Compensation for Environmental Damage* in INTERNATIONAL LEGAL ISSUES ARISING UNDER THE UNITED NATIONS DECADE OF INTERNATIONAL LAW 237–271 (Najeb Al-Nauimi & Richard Meese eds. 1995).

- *Dictionaries*

BALLENTINE'S LAW DICTIONARY 1190 (3d ed.1969).
BLACK'S LAW DICTIONARY 712 (7th ed. 1999).
Yearbooks
Michael Akehurst, *Custom as a Source of International Law*, 47 BRITISH
    Y. INT'L L. 1–53 (1974–75).

- *Internet sources*

Michael Guth, *An Expert System for Curtailing Electric Power*, 2 W. VA.
    J. L. & TECH. 2, 14 (Mar. 1999), at http://www.wvjolt.wvu.edu/v3i2/
    guth.html.

- *Newspapers*

Robert Graham, *Chirac Seeks to Counter US Stance*, FIN. TIMES. Feb.
    11, 2003, at 3.

CHAPTER 9

Special Guidelines for Preparing for the Competition

Take your research and preparation seriously from the beginning and complete all the work in due time; this preparation will pay great dividends when the time comes for the Competition itself

The following is a quick checklist of important elements of successful participation in an international law moot court competition.

Complete the Memorial for Final Submission

Your first job as a team is to complete the Memorial to meet the deadline as required by the rules of the competition. You should do the following:

- Carefully examine the entire Memorial and find the weaknesses.
- Discuss among the team members how the weak portion can be improved and divide the job as the team decides. Include any point that is not covered or discovered later.
- Appoint one member who will make sure that all the formatting rules for Memorial writing are complied with. These rules frequently include word and page limitation, footnote format, size of margins, and special format of the cover page.
- Start your final editing at least one week before the deadline. You should conduct a final formatting check of the entire, finalized Memorial at least two days before the deadline.
- Make sure to comply with the competition rules regarding the deadline and method of delivering the Memorials. Some competitions require certified mail, others require that you get a dated receipt. Read the Memorial delivery rules carefully.

Once you have completed your Memorials and mailed them off, take few days off. Rest is very important. All the team members are normally under a great deal of pressure during the days before submission. Once you have posted the final product, take a few days off.

Preparing for the Oral Round

Once you are rested, you should immediately fix a schedule for oral practice. Consult with your coach and all team members in putting together this schedule. During the practice session, write down the questions asked by the bench and, if new arguments or counter-arguments appear during a practice round, be sure to discuss them with your team.

Some elements of a successful series of practice rounds are as follows:

- Have one or two rounds with a bench not favorable to your position. This bench will be very active and difficult to convince. You might find such a bench during the competition, so this will be good practice.
- Make a video recording of your practice round at least once. You will be able to see how good or terrible you are in action.
- Make sure your bench is able to test the team's basic knowledge of international law.

Make sure to bring the following materials with you to the oral rounds of the competition itself:

- Jessup Compromis, Official Rules and Memorials (yours and your opponents, if available under the rules).
- One public international law casebook.
- One documentary book on basic documents in international law. (for example, *Basic Documents in International Law*, by Burns H. Westin, *et al.*)

Your own notes, research, papers and manuscript.

At the Competition

Keep your goal always in mind and your priority straight. Once you get your opponents' Memorials, go through them and prepare your counter-arguments. Although your opponents are not required to adhere minutely